COWLEY'S ESSAYS

COWLEY'S ESSAYS

EDITED BY

J. RAWSON LUMBY, D.D.

REVISED BY

ARTHUR TILLEY, M.A.

CAMBRIDGE
AT THE UNIVERSITY PRESS
1923

CAMBRIDGE UNIVERSITY PRESS
Cambridge, New York, Melbourne, Madrid, Cape Town,
Singapore, São Paulo, Delhi, Mexico City

Cambridge University Press
The Edinburgh Building, Cambridge CB2 8RU, UK

Published in the United States of America by Cambridge University Press, New York

www.cambridge.org
Information on this title: www.cambridge.org/9781107665279

First edition 1887
Reprinted 1891, 1902
Second edition 1923
First published 1923
First paperback edition 2013

A catalogue record for this publication is available from the British Library

ISBN 978-1-107-66527-9 Paperback

Preface

IN this revision of the Pitt Press edition of Cowley's *Prose Works* I have made considerable changes. I have omitted *A Proposition for the Advancement of Experimental Philosophy, A Discourse by way of Vision concerning the Government of Oliver Cromwell,* and the Preface to *Cutter of Coleman Street*—everything, in short, but the *Discourses by way of Essays.* I have written a new introduction, and I have made the notes much shorter—this last in the interest alike of the young student and the general reader. Most of us have met with young people who have been goaded by superabundant notes into a life-long dislike of some masterpiece. Teachers, publishers, and editors, acting and re-acting upon one another, must all share in the blame. Happily there have been for some time signs of a marked improvement; notes are fewer and shorter, or absent altogether. But there is still too great a tendency in examiners to examine on the notes rather than on the text, and the teacher with his or her finger firmly embedded in the notes is still too common a phenomenon.

All the same, no teacher can be expected to be familiar with every author or, being hard-worked and human, to give sufficient time to the preparation of every lesson. In a seventeenth century author, especially in one like Cowley, who is steeped in classical literature, there must always be archaic words and classical allusions to explain. In these notes, explanation has been my main object, sometimes also illustration. The two longest are a quotation from Pascal and a note on the Toupinambaltians. I don't know that I can justify them, but my young friends will perhaps forgive them in a lover of Pascal and Montaigne.

Both in the introduction and in the notes I have borrowed freely from my learned predecessor, Dr Lumby, especially in the notes for difficulties of language and for illustration from sixteenth and seventeenth century writers. I am also indebted to Mr Gough's excellent edition of Cowley's *Essays and Other Prose Writings*, of which he kindly permitted me to make use, and which for the scholarly study of Cowley will still remain indispensable.

The text, save for one or two unimportant alterations, is that of Mr A. R. Waller's edition of Cowley in the Cambridge English Classics. He hoped at one time to publish a "Supplement of Notes, biographical, bibliographical and critical," but his single-hearted

devotion to the University Press prevented the
realisation of this hope. It is to my lasting regret
that I have been unable to submit to him for criticism
the work which on behalf of the Syndics he entrusted
to me; the leave which he gave me to carry it out in
my own way has turned a task into a pleasure. My
grateful thanks are due to his successor, Mr S. C.
Roberts, who has kindly read the proofs of the
introduction and notes.

A. T.

November 21, 1922

Contents

Introduction

ABRAHAM COWLEY, the seventh and posthumous son of
Thomas Cowley, a stationer domiciled in the parish of
Michael le Querne[1], was born in 1618. Like Milton and
Keats, he was profoundly influenced at an early age by
the poetry of Spenser, a copy of which he found in his
mother's parlour, though "she herself never in her life
read any book but of devotion"[2]. His own poetic faculty
blossomed at a precociously early age, for he was only
ten when he wrote *The Tragical Historie of Pyramus and
Thisbe* in six-lined stanzas, and only twelve when he wrote
Constantia and Philetus in the same metre. They were
published with three other pieces in 1633, when he was at
Westminster School, in a volume entitled *Poetical Blossoms,
Pyramus and Thisbe* being dedicated to Mr Lambert
Osbaldeston, the great Busby's immediate predecessor in
the Headmastership, and *Constantia and Philetus* to the
Dean of Westminster.

Neither the admissions to the School nor those to the
College exist for this period, but Cowley was probably
admitted on the Foundation in 1632, and under the
Statutes of Queen Elizabeth he must have been at the

---

[1] *Notes and Queries*, Series IV, XI. 390. The statement of
Dr Johnson, following Anthony à Wood, that Cowley's father
was a grocer seems to rest on no foundation. St Michael
le Querne, at the extreme east end of Paternoster Row, was
destroyed in the Great Fire and not rebuilt. Sir Thomas
Browne, the author of *Religio Medici*, was baptized in it.
Cowley is usually said to have been born in Fleet Street, near
Temple Bar, and it is possible that his mother removed there
after his father's death.

[2] Essay, *Of My self.*

School at least a year before his admission[1]. In the essay
quoted from above he tells us that

instead of running about on Holy-daies and playing with my
fellows; I was wont to steal from them, and walk into the
fields, either alone with a Book, or with some one Companion,
if I could find any of the same temper. I was then, too, so
much an Enemy to all constraint, that my Masters could
never prevail on me, by any perswasions or encouragements,
to learn without Book the common rules of Grammar, in
which they dispensed with me alone, because they found I
made a shift to do the usual exercise out of my own reading
and observation.

At Westminster Cowley continued to write poetry,
under the approving eye of the Headmaster, who, sharing
to the full the love of his age for far-fetched conceits,
found in the boy an apt pupil. In 1633 Cowley with other
Westminsters celebrated in verse the birth of the Duke
of York[2]. His lines may be compared with those which
Dryden wrote at the same school sixteen years later on
the death of Lord Hastings. The conceits are far more
numerous than in Dryden's poem, and they are not re-
deemed, as the latter is, by any promise of future excellence.

Unfortunately the Electors from Christ Church and
Trinity were more particular than the Westminster
masters about "the common rules of Grammar" and
Cowley failed to obtain a Westminster Scholarship either
at Christ Church or at Trinity. He was admitted to
Trinity as a Pensioner on April 21, 1636[3], and a year
later was elected to an Open Scholarship[4].

[1] I owe this information to my friend Mr G. F. Russell
Barker, the author of *A Memoir of Richard Busby, D.D.* 1895.
See also John Sargeaunt, *Annals of Westminster School*, 1898.
This staunch Johnsonian and inspiring teacher, who for 24 years
was Sixth Form master at Westminster School, died on
March 20, 1922.

[2] Printed by Sargeaunt, *op. cit.* p. 282, from a MS. in the
British Museum entitled *Genethliaca Ducis Eboracensis celebrata
a Musis Reg. Schol. Westmon.*

[3] W. W. Rouse Ball, *Admissions to Trinity College, Cambridge*, 1913, II. 352. [4] He was admitted on June 14, 1637.

Before this he had reprinted his juvenile volume of verse with the addition of *Sylva or Divers Copies of Verses*, and in 1638 he published, with a dedication to Sir Kenelm Digby, a Pastoral Comedy entitled *Love's Riddle*. He also wrote a Latin comedy, *Naufragium joculare*, which was performed in Trinity on February 2, 1638, and four years later he was called upon to provide an English play for the entertainment of the Prince of Wales (the future Charles II), who visited Cambridge on March 12, 1642 (N.S.). It was printed in 1650 under the title of *The Guardian*. Eight years later Cowley re-wrote it, and gave it the new title of *Cutter of Coleman Street*. It was acted in London on December 16, 1661, when Pepys saw it and pronounced it to be "a good play"; it was published in 1663.

At the time of the Prince of Wales's visit to Cambridge Cowley was a B.A. and a Minor Fellow of Trinity, having taken his degree in 1640 (N.S.) and having been admitted to a Fellowship on October 30, 1640. But, though admitted, there was not a Fellowship vacant for him, and in 1643 his name still appears among the Scholars. There is no record of his admission as a Major Fellow[1].

Of his Cambridge friendships the two most notable were those with William Harvey of Pembroke Hall[2] and Richard Crashaw, the poet, who was elected from that College to a Fellowship at Peterhouse in the year in which Cowley came up to Trinity. Their early deaths inspired Cowley with his two best poems. Of Harvey he writes:

> He was my *Friend*, the truest *Friend* on earth;
> A strong and mighty *Influence* joyn'ed our *Birth*.
> * * * * * *
> Say, for you saw us, ye immortal *Lights*.
> How oft unweari'd have we spent the Nights?
> Till the *Ledæan Stars* so famed for *Love*,
> Wondred at us from above.

[1] The particulars from the Trinity College records were given to Dr Lumby by W. Aldis Wright.

[2] William Harvey of Bury St Edmunds was admitted to Pembroke on April 5, 1636, being then in his 17th year. I owe this information to the kindness of Mr Comber, Fellow and Treasurer of Pembroke College.

We spent them not in toys, in lusts, or wine;
        But search of deep *Philosophy,*
        Wit, Eloquence, and *Poetry,*
Arts which I lov'd, for they, my *Friend,* were *Thine.*

Ye fields of *Cambridge,* our dear *Cambridge,* say
Have ye not seen us walking every day?
Was there a *Tree* about which did not know
        The *Love* betwixt us two?
Henceforth, ye gentle *Trees,* for ever fade;
        Or your sad branches thicker joyn,
        And into darksome shades combine,
Dark as the *Grave* wherein my *Friend* is laid.

The elegy on Crashaw, who died at Loreto in 1650, begins:

Poet and *Saint*! to thee alone are given
The two most sacred *Names* of *Earth* and *Heaven,*

and, referring to his friend's having joined the Roman communion, he says:

Pardon, my *Mother Church,* if I consent
That *Angels* led him when from thee he went,
For even in *Error* sure no *Danger* is
When joyn'd with so much *Piety* as *His.*

        *   *   *   *   *   *

His *Faith* perhaps in some nice Tenents might
Be wrong; his *Life,* I'm sure, was in *the right.*
And I my self a *Catholick* will be,
So far at least, great *Saint,* to *Pray* to thee.

In 1643 Cambridge began to suffer from the effects of the Civil War. The Castle was fortified, several of the bridges over the Cam being broken down to provide stone; soldiers were quartered in the colleges; St John's was converted into a prison; outrages were of frequent occurrence. So Cowley migrated to Oxford, where the King had his headquarters, and found hospitality at St John's College. It was apparently at this time that he made the personal acquaintance of Lord Falkland, whom he had long admired, and whose house at Great Tew was within ten miles of Oxford. This

great cherisher of wit and fancy and good parts in any man ...contracted familiarity and friendship with the most polite and accurate men of the university;.who found such an immenseness of wit, such a solidity of judgment in him, so infinite a fancy, such a vast knowledge...that they frequently resorted, and dwelt with him, as in a college situated in a purer air; so that his house was a university bound in a less volume.

But Falkland was now Secretary of State, and during these months of open warfare there can have been little or no opportunity for gatherings at Great Tew, and on September 20, 1643, he sought and found death in the "unhappy battle" of Newbury, leaving an immortal memory which his friend Clarendon has enshrined in some of the noblest pages of our prose[1].

In 1644 the storm descended upon Cambridge with increased severity. For refusing to subscribe to the Covenant, Comber, the Master of Trinity, and 47 Fellows, including Cowley, were ejected from the College; and Cowley's friend Crashaw suffered the same fate at Peterhouse. Cowley himself obtained a post, apparently as secretary, in the household of Lord Jermyn, secretary to Queen Henrietta Maria and commander of her bodyguard. On July 14, 1644, the Queen crossed to France, taking with her Jermyn, and probably Cowley, for Sprat says that Cowley "was absent from his native country for twelve years," and he puts his return in 1656. His service involved him in several "dangerous journies," but he was chiefly employed in ciphering and deciphering the correspondence that passed between the Queen and Charles I, work which "for some years together took up all his day, and two or three nights every week."

In 1656 "it was thought fit," says Sprat, "that he should come over into England, and under pretence of privacy and retirement should take occasion of giving notice of the posture of things in this nation"—a roundabout way of saying that he was sent as a spy. While he lay hid in London, continues Sprat, he was arrested in mistake for some other man, and only released from

---

[1] Clarendon, *History of the Rebellion*, VII. 217–234. Sprat says that Cowley had the entire friendship of Falkland.

custody on the security of the eminent physician Dr Scarborough, who went bail for him for £1000. This is Sprat's story, but Mr A. B. Gough has shewn in his Introduction to his excellent edition of Cowley's *Prose Writings* that it does not tally with the facts. It was really in April 1655, as we learn from *The Weekly Intelligencer* and one or two other newsletters, that "the memorable M. Abraham Cowley, more famous by his pen than by his sword," was arrested in London "for having had a hand in the plot"— that is to say in the Royalist plot which came to an abortive ending in the previous March[1]. Thus Sprat has evidently post-dated Cowley's arrest by a year and is also wrong in his assertion that Cowley was mistaken for another man. Whether he is right in saying that Cowley was sent from France to spy out "the posture of things in this nation," it is impossible to determine. At any rate Cowley, impressed, no doubt, by the rapid fizzling out of the Royalist risings, and apparently released from imprisonment on his promise of good behaviour, seems quietly to have accepted the new Government, in spite of its high-handed and illegal measures. This at least is the inference to be drawn from his preface to a collected edition of such of his poems as he considered worthy of preservation, which he published in 1656. The volume contained: (1) *Miscellanies*, "some of them made when I was very young," (2) *The Mistress*, which had already been published separately in 1647, (3) *Pindarique Odes*, (4) *Davideis*, an heroical poem of the troubles of David in four books, the greater part of which, says Sprat, was written while Cowley was a student at Cambridge. In the preface Cowley explains his reasons for publication and announces his resolution "never to exercise any more the poetical faculty," and in a passage, which was suppressed in subsequent editions of his works, he declares his intention to accept the new order of things:

[1] The Colley whose arrest on or about April 12, 1655, is referred to in *Notes and Queries*, Series IV, xi. 389, is evidently the poet.

When the event of battel, and the unaccountable *Will* of *God* has determined the controversie, and that we have sub-mitted to the conditions of the *Conqueror*, we must lay down our *Pens* as well as *Arms*.... The *enmities* of *Fellow-Citizens* should be, like that of *Lovers*, the *Redintegration* of their *Amity*[1].

Cowley, in short, was not a "Die-hard." Having said farewell (as he thought) to poetry, Cowley gave himself for a time to the study of Medicine and on December 2, 1657, was incorporated in the University of Oxford as a Doctor of Physic. After the death of Cromwell (September 3, 1658) he returned to France and stayed there till just before the Restoration, an event which he celebrated in an Ode of fulsome flattery. Shortly afterwards he was restored to his Fellowship at Trinity, and at the special request of Charles II was granted "the continuance of his seven years before taking holy Orders"[2]. Thus he held his Fellowship till the day of his death.

Cowley now hoped for some substantial recognition of his services to the Royal Family. The Mastership of the Savoy Hospital was said to have been promised to him, but nothing came of it. In a poem entitled *The Complaint*, included in *Verses, Lately Written upon several Occasions* (1663) he refers to himself as "the Melancholy Cowley" and schools himself to bear with patience the still deferred reward of his services.

> Kings have long hands (they say) and though I be
> So distant, they may reach at length to me.

The poem inspired some imitator of Suckling's *Session of the Poets* to write the following stanza:

> Savoy—missing Cowley came into the court,
> Making apologies for his bad play;
> Every one gave him so good a report,
> That Apollo gave heed to all he could say:

[1] Sprat says, "he was a close prisoner when he wrote this," but, seeing Sprat's confusion of dates, it is difficult to accept this statement.

[2] Trinity Admission Book, under date of February 11, 1661 (N.S.).

>   Nor would he have had, 'tis thought, a rebuke,
>   Unless he had done some notable folly;
>   Writ verses unjustly in praise of Sam Tuke,
>   Or printed his pitiful Melancholy[1].

In 1662 the Royal Society was incorporated by Charter and Cowley became one of its original members. A few years earlier—before his return to France after the Protector's death—he had written *A Proposition for the Advancement of Experimental Philosophy*, which consists of a fully detailed scheme for the foundation of a Philosophical College. It was discussed by the Royal Society in November 1660[2] and published in the following year. Though Cowley's studies for his medical degree seem to have been more or less confined to botanising in Kent[3], he shared to the full the interest in science taken by the leading men of his day; his *Ode upon Dr Harvey* which he included in the *Verses* of 1663 and the *Ode to the Royal Society*, which he wrote in 1667, though only here and there they rise to real poetry, are not the worst of his more ambitious poems.

In 1663, the Mastership of the Savoy Hospital having been given to another, Cowley put into execution the design he had been for some time meditating of "withdrawing himself from all tumult and business of the world"[4]. He was the better able to do this because through the good offices of Lord St Albans (Lord Jermyn) the Duke of Buckingham had bought and presented to him a lease of the Queen-Mother's lands at Chertsey on terms so favourable as to promise him a net income of £300 a year[5]. He first retired to Barn Elms, near Putney, then a favourite resort of Londoners, and here Evelyn

---

[1] Quoted by Johnson in his *Life of Cowley*. In the *Dict. of Nat. Biog.* the lines are attributed to Suckling himself, who died in 1642.

[2] See Gough, *op. cit.* p. 242.

[3] In 1662 he published *Plantarum libri duo* in Latin verse.

[4] Essay X, *The Danger of Procrastination*.

[5] The most explicit account of this transaction is given by Aubrey and reproduced by Stebbing.

visited his "excellent and ingenious friend" on May 14, 1663, paying him another visit on January 2, 1664, "after his sickness." In April 1665 Cowley moved to the Porch House, Chertsey, which still stands, though deprived of its porch. His first experiences in his new home were unfortunate, as we may see from the following letter to his friend Thomas Sprat, afterwards Dean of Westminster and Bishop of Worcester.

Chertsey, May 21, 1665.

The first night that I came hither I caught so great a cold, with a defluxion of rheum, as made me keep my chamber ten days. And, two after, had such a bruise on my ribs with a fall, that I am yet unable to move or turn myself in my bed. This is my personal fortune here to begin with. And, besides, I can get no money from my tenants, and have my meadows eaten up every night by cattle put in by my neighbours. What this signifies, or may come to in time, God knows; if it be ominous, it can end in nothing less than hanging. Another misfortune has been, and stranger than all the rest, that you have broke your word with me, and failed to come, even though you told Mr Bois that you would. This is what they call "Monstri simile." I do hope to recover my late hurt so farre within five or six days, (though it be uncertain yet whether I shall ever recover it,) as to walk about again. And then, methinks, you and I and "the dean" might be very merry upon St Ann's hill. You might very conveniently come hither the way of Hampton Town, lying there one night. I write this in pain, and can say no more: "Verbum sapienti"[1].

After reading this we can easily believe Sprat when he tells us that Cowley excelled in his letters to his private friends, and we cannot sufficiently condemn Sprat for declining to publish them, on the ground that "in such Letters the Souls of Men should appear undressed." "What literary man," asks Coleridge "has not regretted the prudery of Sprat in refusing to let his friend Cowley appear in his slippers and dressing gown?"

During the last leisured years of his life Cowley wrote

---

[1] Printed in Johnson's *Life of Cowley*.

but little—a few poems, eleven short essays, to which
he appended some verse translations from the Latin
poets, and some more books of plants in Latin verses,
making the whole number up to six. He planned various
works—"a discourse concerning style" of which his
friend Sprat could find no traces but "some indigested
Characters of Ancient and Modern Authors," and a
history of the Church during the first four or five centuries,
and "it was his design to have added many other essays."
But none of these pleasant projects came to fruition. He
was again taken ill, and "languished for some months."
Then he seemed to be "pretty well cured," but in the
summer of 1667 a neglected cold developed into a serious
illness, and he died on July 28, in the forty-ninth year
of his age. Four days later Evelyn records in his diary
that he "receiv'd the sad news of Abraham Cowley's
death, that incomparable poet and virtuous man, my
very dear friend," and Charles II declared that "Mr Cowley
had not left a better man behind him in England." The
funeral ceremony on August 3 testified to the honour in
which he was held. His body, writes Evelyn, "was
convey'd to Westminster Abbey in a hearse with 6 horses
and all funeral decency, near an hundred coaches of noble-
men and persons of quality following; among these all the
wits of the town, divers bishops and clergymen. He was
interred next Geoffrey Chaucer, and near to Spenser."
Denham wrote his elegy, the Duke of Buckingham erected
his monument, and Sprat composed the inscription,
"Anglorum Pindarus, Flaccus, Maro, Deliciae, Decus,
Desiderium Aevi sui"—so it runs—and to justify this
perfervid *elogium* Sprat published in 1668 an edition of his
friend's works with a prefatory account of his life and
writings. Unfortunately it contains a small modicum of
fact to an "intolerable deal" of sentiment.

Cowley "lisped in numbers," but nature meant him to
be a prose-writer rather than a poet, for reason not
imagination was his mistress. He had wit, ingenuity,
learning, understanding, all admirable qualities in a

writer of prose; but lacking the wings of imagination and the driving-power of passion, he could not fly. His most ambitious attempts at flight—his *Davideis*, his *Pindarique Odes*—are his worst failures. Even the Odes *To Mr Hobs* and *To the Royal Society*, which some have praised highly, are little more than fine declamations in praise of philosophy and science. Confront them with the *Hymn on the Nativity* by Cowley's great contemporary, and they are at once detected as impostors. It is only when sincerity constrains him to be simple that Cowley is a real poet, as in the elegies on his friends William Harvey and the poet Crashaw.

On the other hand, he is a delightful prose writer. Moreover he is of singular interest, for, with Dryden, he marks the beginning of the new post-Restoration prose, with its lucid thought, short periods, and easy conversational tone. He failed in poetry, partly because having little real imagination he tried to write in the lofty style, rich in imagery, appropriate to Pindaric and other odes, partly because in compliance with contemporary fashion and under the influence of Lambert Osbaldeston he indulged in tasteless conceits. But he was a clear and orderly thinker and a man of genuine simplicity, so that, when he descended to prose, he was by nature disposed towards a style which demanded these qualities.

He could not of course shake off in a moment the methods and mannerisms of Caroline prose. In the preface of 1656 his sentences are cumbrous and involved, with a tendency to trailing sequences of relatives, and it is only in the last three or four pages that they become shorter and better balanced. The Preface to *A Proposition for the Advancement of Experimental Philosophy*, which was written in 1659, shews a decided progress, but it has one or two unwieldy sentences. The *Vision concerning Cromwell*, written in 1658 or 1659, and published in 1661, belongs, as might be expected from its character, more decidedly to the older school, and the latter part of it is a fine example of rhetorical prose. Even in the

Preface to *Cutter of Coleman Street* (1663), though the
sentences are, as a rule, short and well balanced, Cowley
has by no means wholly eradicated the faults of the
older style. Then we came to the essays proper, eleven
in number, which he wrote during the last four or five
years of his life. The date of some of them can be approxi-
mately fixed, and of all it can be conjectured within no
very wide limits. Thus *The Garden* (5) must belong to
1666, for it was in answer to Evelyn's dedication to
Cowley of the second edition of his *Kalendarium Hortense*.
Of Obscurity (3) must have been written in 1666 or 1667,
for Browne's translation of Horace was not published
till the former year. *The Danger of an Honest man in
much Company* (8) was written at Chertsey. *The Danger
of Procrastination* (10) is one of the earliest, for Cowley
had not yet accomplished his design of withdrawing from
the world. On the other hand in the last, *Of My self*, he
says that "he met...with so much sickness as would
have spoiled the happiness of an emperor as well as mine,"
which, with its reference to "these precedent discourses,"
suggests that it was written in 1666 after his third illness.
It is more of a conjecture that the meditation on *The
Shortness of Life* was provoked by one of these illnesses.
In the remaining five essays there are no references to
events to enable us to determine their date, but in two
of them, *Of Solitude* (2) and *Of Greatness* (6), Cowley cites
Montaigne, borrowing from him the titles[1] and some of
the contents of these essays.

It is possible that Cowley may have read Montaigne
in France, for during the years of his sojourn there the
great essayist was exceedingly popular. But the English,
with the exception of Hobbes, seem to have had little
intercourse with French society and French men of letters,
and it is far more likely that Saint-Évremond, who made
England his home from 1662 to 1665 and from 1670
to his death, and who was on intimate terms with

[1] *De la solitude* (I. 38) and *De l'incommodité de la grandeur*
(III. 7).

the English wits and courtiers, introduced Cowley to Montaigne. At any rate the influence of Montaigne on Cowley is unmistakeable not only in these two essays, but on all those, except *The Danger of Procrastination*, for which a date has been suggested. On the other hand, in the three essays not yet mentioned, *Of Liberty*, *Of Agriculture*, and *Of Avarice*, the personal element which is so eminently characteristic of Montaigne, is entirely lacking, while in *The Danger of Procrastination* it only peeps forth at the beginning of the essay, and after that keeps discretely in the background. The inference is that these four essays are the earliest. The essays then may be conjecturally arranged in order of composition as follows: (1) *Of Agriculture*, (2) *Of Liberty*, (3) *Of Avarice*, (4) *The Danger of Procrastination*, (5) *Of Solitude*, (6) *Of Greatness*, (7) *The Dangers of an Honest man in much Company*, (8) *The Shortness of Life*, (9) *The Garden*, (10) *Of Obscurity*, (11) *Of My self*.

The essays *Of Agriculture* and *Of Liberty* are clearly the earliest. They are rather longer than any of the others and they exhibit in places the defects of the older style. *Of Agriculture* seems to be the earlier of the two, partly because it is closely connected in its subject matter with *A Proposition for the Advancement of Experimental Philosophy*, and partly because the long sentences predominate. Indeed the sentence on pp. 34–35, "The utility etc.," is not only extremely long, but unwieldy and formless into the bargain. We have three relative clauses ("the reason of *which* I conceive"...as if it were a law, "*which* is....but such *who* are so poor"), followed by another long dependent clause ("that...the tenant"); and finally there is tacked on at the end a fresh clause, introduced by *whilst* and then qualified by *though*. The sentence on p. 38, "All these considerations etc.," though rather shorter, is even worse in point of construction. We may note too the rhetorical turn of the passage from "We are here among the vast and noble Scenes of Nature"; to "there guilty and expenseful Luxury,"

(p. 37), with its succession of formal antitheses—quite unlike the simplicity of Cowley's later essays and strangely
anticipatory of Johnson.

So too in the essay *Of Liberty* we find a very long
sentence on p. 4 ("Above all things etc."), a badly con-
structed one on p. 12 ("The Voluptuous Man etc.") and
one with a double relative clause on p. 13 ("This by the
Calumniators of Epicurus etc."). Even in *The Danger of
Procrastination* there is a sentence of considerable length:
"The summ of this is...Top-Gallants" (pp. 103–104). But
here it is chiefly a question of punctuation; by putting a
a full stop after "recovered" and another after "candle,"
we can break it up into three short and excellent sentences.
The essay *Of Avarice* is in a different style; its brevity
and sententiousness shew that Cowley is experimenting
in the manner of Bacon. But when we come to the two
essays in which Montaigne is mentioned, we meet with an
almost new type of essay. One of Montaigne's charac-
teristics, the quotations and 'examples' from classical
authors, Cowley possessed already, but he owes to his new
model the combination of a conversational ease of tone
with artistic workmanship, and the personal element.
And it is just this personal element which saves Cowley
from being a mere satellite of Montaigne. In the words
of his biographer, his essays are "a real Character of his
own Thoughts upon the Point of his Retirement." They
reflect too the qualities ascribed to him by his friend—his
lack of affectation, his modesty and humility, and, above
all, the pleasant gravity of his speech. But let Sprat
speak for himself:

There was nothing affected or singular in his Habit, or
Person, or Gesture. He understood the Forms of good Breeding
enough to practise them without burdening himself, or
others....His Modesty and Humility were so great, that if
he had not had many other equal Virtues, they might have
been thought Dissimulation. His Conversation was certainly
of the most excellent kind for it was such as was rather admired
by his familiar Friends, than by Strangers at first sight....In
his Speech, neither the Pleasantness excluded Gravity, nor

was the Sobriety of it inconsistent with Delight.... His
Learning was large and profound, well compos'd of all Ancient
and Modern Knowledge. But it sate exceeding close and
handsomly upon him. It was not imboss'd on his Mind, but
enamell'd.... He was a passionate Lover of Liberty, and
Freedom from Restraint both in Actions and Words. But
what Honesty others receive from the Direction of Laws, he
had by native Inclination: And he was not beholding to other
Mens Wills, but to his own for his Innocence.

Finally Sprat speaks, though without applauding it,
of Cowley's "earnest Affection for Obscurity and Retirement," and this is practically the theme of all his last
seven essays. In the essay *Of Solitude* he begins by quoting
from Cicero a saying which Cato attributed to Scipio
Africanus, that "One is never less alone than when alone."
This brings him to Seneca's description of Scipio's villa
at Liternum. Then he cites a sentence from Montaigne's
essay *On Solitude* that "Ambition it self might teach us
to love Solitude; there's nothing does so much hate to
have Companions." To this he adds his own comment.
"'Tis true," he says, "it loves to have its Elbows free
(*ses coudées franches*)... but it delights above all Things
in a Train behind, I (aye), and Ushers too before it."
(Note how Cowley plays up to Montaigne's metaphor.)
Then he compares the majority of mankind to "a becalmed Ship; they never move but by the wind of other
mens breath, and have no Oars of their own to steer
withal." There follow quotations from Horace, Tibullus,
and Catullus. But solitude is only suited to a very few
persons—not to those who are possessed by passions, for
these like robbers murder us when they catch us alone.
For a man to enjoy solitude he must first eradicate all
lusts; secondly he must get the habit of thinking; and
in order to get this he must have continual recourse to
learning and books.

The essay *Of Greatness* opens with a quotation from
Montaigne and towards the end there are two almost
certain reminiscences of him. And the whole essay is

more in Montaigne's manner than its companion; it has more vivacity, more nimbleness, more ease; it digresses, it dallies on the way, instead of making straight for its goal. There is an anecdote freely translated from the elder Seneca; there are a few examples from Suetonius of the foibles of Roman emperors; there is a pointed reference to "the late Gyant of our Nation"; a quotation or two from the Latin poets; and a few lines of the author's own.

For the remaining five essays it is enough to point out that the fact of *The Garden* being addressed to that eminent dilettante, John Evelyn, accounts for a more ceremonial style and perhaps for the conceit that horti-culture is Evelyn's wife and the other arts his concubines; that *The Shortness of Life* is written in a graver tone, as befits the subject; and that in the admirable essay *Of My self*, which one is tempted to regard as the latest of all, and which at any rate is Cowley's crowning achieve-ment, he gives full expression to that personal note which is so delightful a characteristic of his latest essays.

The posthumous volume of 1668 had a great success, and in 1721 reached a twelfth edition. In 1737 Pope in his *Epistle to Augustus* asks "Who now reads Cowley?"; but he was thinking of his poetry and in the charming edition in two volumes of his *Select Works* which Richard Hurd, afterwards Bishop of Worcester, published in 1772, the editor declares that "the Sieur de Montagne and Mr Cowley are our two great models of essay-writing." Fifty years later two of the greatest of English essayists acted on this belief. In the *Round Table* we find Hazlitt declaring his preference for the *Tatler* over the *Spectator* and "all the periodical Essayists (our ingenious pre-decessors)." Is this because the personal element is more prominent in the *Tatler* than in the rest? But though Steele recounts his own experiences, he does not admit us to his intimacy. Nor indeed does Hazlitt in the *Round Table* essays (1815–1817). The three earliest at-tempts of Elia are personal reminiscences rather than true essays. But in the December number of the *London*

INTRODUCTION xxvii

Magazine for 1820, which contains Lamb's *The two races of Men* and Hazlitt's *The pleasures of painting*, the personal essay comes to its own. Lamb and Hazlitt handled it with a variety and a gusto unknown to Cowley, but when we surrender ourselves to the charm of their delightful art, let us in justice remember that (so far as English literature is concerned) it was Cowley who created the type.

PRINCIPAL EDITIONS OF COWLEY'S PROSE WRITINGS

1. In *Works*, fo. 1668; 9th ed. fo. 1700; 10th ed. 3 vols. 8vo. 1707–1708; 11th ed. 3 vols. 8vo. 1710–1711; 12th ed. 3 vols. 12mo. 1721.

2. *Select Works*, with preface and notes [by R. Hurd], 2 vols. 1772.

3. *Essays, Plays and Sundry Verses*, ed. A. R. Waller. Cambridge, 1906.

4. *Essays and Other Prose Writings*, ed. Alfred B. Gough. Oxford, 1915.

LIFE AND CRITICISMS

1. Account of life and writings prefixed by Thomas Sprat to the 1668 edition of the *Works*.

2. Samuel Johnson, *Lives of the English Poets*, 1779–1781.

3. *Encyclopædia Britannica*. (By Leslie Stephen.)

4. *Dictionary of National Biography*. (By Edmund Gosse.)

5. W. Stebbing, *Verdicts of History Reviewed*, 1887.

6. A. W. Fox, *A Book of Bachelors*, 1899.

7. A. B. Gough, Biographical Sketch, prefixed to his edition of the *Essays*.

Several Discourses by way of Essays, in Verse and Prose

1. *Of Liberty.*

THE Liberty of a people consists in being governed by Laws which they have made themselves, under whatsoever form it be of Government. The Liberty of a private man in being Master of his own Time and Actions, as far as may consist with the Laws of God and of his Country. Of this latter only we are here to discourse, and to enquire what estate of Life does best seat us in the possession of it. This Liberty of our own Actions is such a Fundamental Priviledge of human Nature, that God himself notwithstanding all his infinite power and right over us, permits us to enjoy it, and that too after a Forfeiture made by the Rebellion of *Adam*. He takes so much care for the intire preservation of it to us, that he suffers neither his Providence nor Eternal Decree to break or infringe it. Now for our Time, the same God, to whom we are but Tenants-at-will for the whole, requires but the seventh part to be paid to him as a small Quit-Rent in acknowledgment of his Title. It is man only that has the impudence to demand our whole time, though he neither gave it, nor can restore it, nor is able to pay any considerable valew for the least part of it. This Birth-right of mankind above all other creatures, some

are forced by hunger to sell, like *Esau*, for Bread and
Broth, but the greatest part of men make such a
Bargain for the delivery up of themselves, as *Thamar*
did with *Judah*, instead of a Kid, the necessary provisions for humane life, they are contented to do it
for Rings and Bracelets. The great dealers in this world
may be divided into the Ambitious, the Covetous, and
the Voluptuous, and that all these men sell themselves
to be slaves, though to the vulgar it may seem a Stoical
Paradox, will appear to the wise so plain and obvious
that they will scarce think it deserves the labour of
Argumentation. Let us first consider the Ambitious,
and those both in their progress to Greatness, and
after the attaining of it. There is nothing truer than
what *Salust* saies, *Dominationis in alios servitium suum
Mercedem dant*, They are content to pay so great a
price as their own Servitude to purchase the domina-
tion over others. The first thing they must resolve to
sacrifice, is their whole time, they must never stop,
nor ever turn aside whilst they are in the race of
Glory, no not like *Atalanta* for Golden Apples. Neither
indeed can a man stop himself if he would when he's
in this Career. *Fertur equis Auriga neque audit Currus
habenas.*

Pray, let us but consider a little, what mean servil
things men do for this Imaginary Food. We cannot
fetch a greater example of it, then from the chief men
of that Nation which boasted most of Liberty. To
what pitiful baseness did the noblest *Romans* submit
themselves for the obtaining of a Prætorship, or the
Consular dignity: they put on the Habit of Suppliants,

and ran about on foot, and in dürt, through all the Tribes to beg voices, they flattered the poorest Artisans, and carried a *Nomenclator* with them, to whisper in their ear every mans name, least they should mistake it in their salutations: they shook the hand, and kist the cheek of every popular Tradesman; they stood all day at every Market in the publick places to shew and ingratiate themselves to the rout; they imploy'd all their friends to sollicite for them, they kept open Tables in every street, they distributed wine and bread and money, even to the vilest of the people. *En Romanos rerum Dominos! Behold the Masters of the World begging from door to door.* This particular humble way to Greatness is now out of fashion, but yet every Ambitious person is still in some sort a *Roman* Candidate. He must feast and bribe, and attend and flatter, and adore many Beasts, though not the Beast with many heads. *Catiline* who was so proud that he could not content himself with a less power than *Sylla's*, was yet so humble for the attaining of it, as to make himself the most contemptible of all Servants, to be a publique Bawd, to provide whores, and something worse, for all the young Gentlemen of *Rome*, whose hot lusts and courages, and heads he thought he might make use of. And since I happen here to propose *Catiline* for my instance (though there be thousand of Examples for the same thing) give me leave to transcribe the Character which *Cicero* gives of this noble Slave, because it is a general description of all Ambitious men, and which *Machiavil* perhaps would say ought to be the rule of their life and actions. This man (saies he, as most of you may well remember) had many artificial touches and stroakes that look'd like the beauty of great Virtues, his intimate conversation was with the worst of men, and yet he seem'd to be an Admirer and Lover of the best, he was furnish't with all the nets of Lust and Luxury, and yet wanted not the Arms of Labour and Industry: neither do I believe that there was ever any monster in nature, composed out of so many different and disagreeing parts. Who more acceptable, sometimes, to the most honorable persons, who more a favourite to the most Infamous? who, sometimes, appear'd a braver Champion, who at other times, a bolder Enemy to his Country? who more dissolute in his pleasures, who more patient in his toiles? who more rapacious in robbing, who more profuse in giving? Above all things, this was remarkable and admirable in him, The arts he had to acquire the good opinion and kindness of all sorts of men, to retain it with great complaisance, to communicate all things to them, to watch and serve all the occasions of their fortune, both with his money and his interest, and his industry; and if need were, not by sticking at any wickedness whatsoever that might be useful to them, to bend and turn about his own Nature and laveer with every wind, to live severely with the melancholy, merrily with the pleasant, gravely with the aged, wantonly with the young, desperately with the bold, and debauchedly with the luxurious: with this variety and multiplicity of his nature, as he had made a collection of friendships with all the most wicked and reckless of all Nations, so by the artificial simulation

of some vertues, he made a shift to ensnare some
honest and eminent persons into his familiarity; neither
could so vast a design as the destruction of this Empire
have been undertaken by him, if the immanity of so
many vices had not been covered and disguised by the
appearances of some excellent qualities.

I see, methinks, the Character of an *Anti-Paul*, who
became all things to all men, that he might destroy
all; who only wanted the assistance of Fortune to have
been as great as his Friend *Cæsar* was a little after
him. And the ways of *Cæsar* to compass the same
ends (I mean till the Civil War, which was but another
manner of setting his Country on Fire) were not unlike
these, though he used afterward his unjust Dominion
with more moderation then I think the other would
have done. *Salust* therefore who was well acquainted
with them both, and with many such like Gentlemen
of his time, saies, That it is the nature of Ambition
(*Ambitio multos mortales falsos fieri coegit &*) to make
men Lyers and Cheaters, to hide the Truth in their
breasts, and show, like juglers, another thing in their
Mouths, to cut all friendships and enmities to the
measure of their own Interest, and to make a good
Countenance without the help of good will. And can
there be Freedom with this perpetual constraint? What
is it but a kind of Rack that forces men to say what
they have no mind to? I have wondred at the extravagant and barbarous stratagem of *Zopirus*, and more
at the praises which I finde of so deformed an action;
who though he was one of the seven Grandees of
Persia, and the Son of *Megabises*, who had freed before

his Country from an ignoble Servitude, slit his own
Nose and Lips, cut off his own Ears, scourged and
wounded his whole body, that he might, under pretence
of having been mangled so inhumanly by *Darius*, be
received into *Babylon* (then beseiged by the *Persians*)
and get into the command of it by the recommenda-
tion of so cruel a Sufferance, and their hopes of his
endeavouring to revenge it. It is great pity the *Baby-
lonians* suspected not his falshood, that they might
have cut off his hands too, and whipt him back again.
But the design succeeded, he betrayed the City, and
was made Governour of it. What brutish master ever
punished his offending Slave with so little mercy as
Ambition did this *Zopirus*? and yet how many are
there in all nations who imitate him in some degree
for a less reward? who though they indure not so
much corporal pain for a small preferment or some
honour (as they call it) yet stick not to commit actions,
by which they are more shamefully and more lastingly
stigmatized? But you may say, Though these be the
most ordinary and open waies to greatness, yet there
are narrow, thorney, and little-trodden paths too,
through which some men finde a passage by vertuous
industry. I grant, sometimes they may; but then that
Industry must be such, as cannot consist with Liberty,
though it may with Honesty.

   Thou'rt careful, frugal, painful; we commend a
Servant so, but not a Friend.

   Well then, we must acknowledg the toil and
drudgery which we are forced to endure in this Ascent,
but we are Epicures and Lords when once we are

gotten up into the High Places. This is but a short
Apprentiship after which we are made free of a Royal
Company. If we fall in love with any beautious woman,
we must be content that they should be our Mistresses
whilst we woo them, as soon as we are wedded and
enjoy, 'tis we shall be the Masters.

I am willing to stick to this similitude in the case of
Greatness; we enter into the Bonds of it, like those
of Matrimony; we are bewitcht with the outward and
painted Beauty, and take it for Better or worse, before
we know its true nature and interiour Inconveniences.
A great Fortune (saies *Seneca*) is a great servitude, But
many are of that Opinion which *Brutus* imputes (I hope
untruly) even to that Patron of Liberty, his Friend
Cicero, We fear (saies he to *Atticus*) Death, and Banishment, and Poverty, a great deal too much. *Cicero*, I
am afraid, thinks these to be the worst of evils, and
if he have but some persons, from whom he can obtain
what he has a mind to, and others who will flatter
and worship him, seems to be well enough contented
with an honorable servitude, if any thing indeed ought
to be called honorable, in so base and contumelious
a condition. This was spoken as became the bravest
man who was ever born in the bravest Commonwealth:
But with us generally, no condition passes for servitude,
that is accompanied with great riches, with honors,
and with the service of many Inferiours. This is but
a Deception of the sight through a false medium, for
if a Groom serve a Gentleman in his chamber, that
Gentleman a Lord, and that Lord a Prince; The Groom,
the Gentleman, and the Lord, are as much servants

one as the other: the circumstantial difference of the
ones getting only his Bread and wages, the second a
plentiful, and the third a superfluous estate, is no
more intrinsical to this matter then the difference
between a plain, a rich and gaudy Livery. I do not
say, That he who sells his whole time, and his own
will for one hundred thousand, is not a wiser Merchant
than he who does it for one hundred pounds, but I
will swear, they are both Merchants, and that he is
happier than both, who can live contentedly without
selling that estate to which he was born. But this
Dependance upon Superiours is but one chain of the
Lovers of Power, *Amatorem Trecentæ Pirithoum cohi-
bent catenæ.* Let's begin with him by break of day:
For by that time he's besieged by two or three hundred
Suitors; and the Hall and Antichambers (all the Out-
works) possest by the Enemy as soon as his Chamber
opens, they are ready to break into that, or to corrupt
the Guards, for entrance. This is so essential a part
of Greatness, that whosoever is without it, looks like
a Fallen Favorite, like a person disgraced, and condemned to do what he please all the morning. There
are some who rather then want this, are contented to
have their rooms fild up every day with murmuring
and cursing Creditors, and to charge bravely through
a Body of them to get to their Coach. Now I would
fain know which is the worst duty, that of any one
particular person who waits to speak with the Great
man, or the Great mans, who waits every day to
speak with all the company. *Aliena negotia centum
Per caput & circum saliunt latus,* A hundred businesses

of other men (many unjust and most impertinent) fly
continually about his Head and Ears, and strike him
in the Face like Dorres; Let's contemplate him a
little at another special Scene of Glory, and that is,
his Table. Here he seems to be the Lord of all Nature:
The Earth affords him her best Metals for his dishes,
her best Vegetables and Animals for his food; the Air
and Sea supply him with their choicest Birds and
Fishes: and a great many men who look like Masters,
attend upon him, and yet when all this is done, even
all this is but Table d'Hoste, 'Tis crowded with people
for whom he cares not, for with many Parasites, and
some Spies, with the most burdensome sort of Guests,
the Endeavourers to be witty.

But every body pays him great respect, every body
commends his Meat, that is, his Mony; every body
admires the exquisite dressing & ordering of it, that
is, his Clark of the kitchin, or his Cook; every body
loves his Hospitality, that is, his Vanity. But I desire
to know why the honest In-keeper who provides a
publick Table for his Profit, should be but of a mean
profession; and he who does it for his Honour, a
munificent Prince, You'l say, Because one sels, and
the other gives: Nay, both sell, though for different
things, the one for plain Money, the other for I know
not what Jewels, whose value is in Custom and in
Fancy. If then his Table be made a Snare (as the
Scripture speakes) to his Liberty, where can he hope
for Freedom, there is alwaies, and every where some
restraint upon him. He's guarded with Crowds, and
shackled with Formalities. The half hat, the whole hat,

the half smile, the whole smile, the nod, the embrace,
the Positive parting with a little bow, the Comparative
at the middle of the room, the Superlative at the door;
and if the person be *Pan huper sebastus*, there's a
Hupersuperlative ceremony then of conducting him to
the bottome of the stairs, or to the very gate: as if
there were such Rules set to these *Leviathans* as are
to the Sea, *Hitherto shalt thou go, and no further.*
Perditur hæc inter miseros Lux, Thus wretchedly the
precious day is lost.

How many impertinent Letters and Visits must he
receive, and sometimes answer both too as imper-
tinently? he never sets his foot beyond his Threshold,
unless, like a Funeral, he have a train to follow him,
as if, like the dead Corps, he could not stir, till the
Bearers were all ready. My life, (sayes *Horace*, speaking
to one of these *Magnifico's*) is a great deal more easie
and commodious then thine, In that I can go into
the Market and cheapen what I please without being
wondred at; and take my Horse and ride as far as
Tarentum, without being mist. 'Tis an unpleasant constraint to be alwayes under the sight and observation,
and censure of others; as there may be Vanity in it,
so methinks, there should be Vexation too of spirit:
And I wonder how Princes can endure to have two
or three hundred men stand gazing upon them whilst
they are at dinner, and taking notice of every bit they
eat. Nothing seems greater and more Lordly then the
multitude of Domestick Servants; but, even this too,
if weighed seriously, is a piece of Servitude; unless you
will be a Servant to them (as many men are) the

trouble and care of yours in the Government of them all, is much more then that of every one of them in their observance of you. I take the Profession of a School-Master to be one of the most usefull, and which ought to be of the most honourable in a Commonwealth, yet certainly all his Fasces and Tyrannical Authority over so many Boys, takes away his own Liberty more than theirs.

I do but slightly touch upon all these particulars of the slavery of Greatness: I shake but a few of their outward Chains; their Anger, Hatred, Jealousie, Fear, Envy, Grief, and all the *Etcætera* of their Passions, which are the secret, but constant Tyrants and Torturers of their life, I omit here, because though they be symptomes most frequent and violent in this Disease; yet they are common too in some degree to the Epidemical Disease of Life it self. But, the Ambitious man, though he be so many wayes a slave (*O toties servus!*) yet he bears it bravely and heroically; he struts and looks big upon the Stage; he thinks himself a real Prince in his Masking Habit, and deceives too all the foolish part of his Spectators: He's a slave in *Saturnalibus.* The Covetous Man is a downright Servant, a Draught Horse without Bells or Feathers; *ad Metalla damnatus*, a man condemned to work in Mines, which is the lowest and hardest condition of servitude; and, to encrease his Misery, a worker there for he knows not whom: He heapeth up Riches and knows not who shall enjoy them; 'Tis onely sure that he himself neither shall nor can injoy them. He's an indigent needy slave, he will hardly allow himself

Cloaths, and Board-Wages; *Unciatim vix demenso de suo suum defraudans Genium comparsit miser*; He defrauds not only other Men, but his own Genius; He cheats himself for Mony. But the servile and miserable condition of this wretch is so apparent, that I leave it, as evident to every mans sight, as well as judgment. It seems a more difficult work to prove that the Voluptuous Man too is but a servant: What can be more the life of a Freeman, or as we say ordinarily, of a Gentleman, then to follow nothing but his own pleasures? Why, I'le tell you who is that true Freeman, and that true Gentleman; Not he who blindly follows all his pleasures (the very name of Follower is servile) but he who rationally guides them, and is not hindred by outward impediments in the conduct and enjoyment of them. If I want skill or force to restrain the Beast that I ride upon, though I bought it, and call it my own, yet in the truth of the matter I am at that time rather his Man, then he my Horse. The Voluptuous Men (whom we are fallen upon) may be divided, I think, into the Lustful and Luxurious, who are both servants of the Belly; the other whom we spoke of before, the Ambitious and the Covetous, were κακὰ θηρία, Evil wilde Beasts, these are Γαστέρες ἀργαί, slow Bellies, as our Translation renders it; but the word Ἀργαὶ (which is a fantastical word, with two directly opposite significations) will bear as well the translation of Quick or Diligent Bellies, and both Interpretations may be applyed to these men. *Metrodorus* said, That he had learnt Ἀληθῶς γαστρὶ χαρίζε-σθαι, to give his Belly just thanks for all his pleasures.

This by the Calumniators of *Epicurus* his Philosophy was objected as one of the most scandalous of all their sayings; which, according to my Charitable understanding may admit a very virtuous sence, which is, that he thanked his own Belly for that moderation in the customary appetites of it, which can only give a Man Liberty and Happiness in this World. Let this suffice at present to be spoken of those great Triumviri of the World; the Covetous Man, who is a mean villain, like *Lepidus*; the Ambitious, who is a brave one, like *Octavius*, and the Voluptuous, who is a loose and debauched one, like *Mark Antony*. *Quisnam igitur Liber? Sapiens, sibi qui Imperiosus:* Not *Oenomaus*, who commits himself wholly to a Chariotteer that may break his Neck, but the Man,

> Who governs his own course with steddy hand,
> Who does Himself with Sovereign Pow'r command;
> Whom neither Death, nor Poverty does fright,
> Who stands not aukwardly in his own light
> Against the Truth: who can when Pleasures knock
> Loud at his door, keep firm the bolt and lock.
> Who can though Honour at his gate should stay
> In all her Masking Cloaths, send her away,
> And cry, be gone, I have no mind to Play.

This I confess is a Freeman: but it may be said, That many persons are so shackled by their Fortune, that they are hindred from enjoyment of that Manumission which they have obtained from Virtue. I do both understand, and in part feel the weight of this objection: All I can Answer to it, is, That we must get as much Liberty as we can, we must use our utmost endeavours, and when all that is done, be contented with the Length of that Line which is allow'd us. If you ask me in what condition of Life I think the most allow'd; I should pitch upon that sort of People whom King *James* was wont to call the Happiest of our Nation, the Men placed in the Countrey by their Fortune above an High-Constable, and yet beneath the trouble of a Justice of Peace, in a moderate plenty, without any just argument for the desire of encreasing it by the care of many relations, and with so much knowledge and love of Piety and Philosophy (that is of the study of Gods Laws, and of his Creatures) as may afford him matter enough never to be Idle though without Business; and never to be Melancholy though without Sin or Vanity.

I shall conclude this tedious Discourse with a Prayer of mine in a Copy of Latin Verses, of which I remember no other part, and (*pour faire bonne bouche*) with some other Verses upon the same Subject.

Magne Deus, quod ad has vitæ brevis attinet horas,
Da mihi, da Panem Libertatemque, nec ultrà
Sollicitas effundo preces, siquid datur ultrà
Accipiam gratus; si non, Contentus abibo.

For the few Houres of Life allotted me,
Give me (great God) but Bread and Liberty,
I'le beg no more; if more thou'rt pleas'd to give,
I'le thankfully that Overplus receive:
If beyond this no more be freely sent,
I'le thank for this, and go away content.

Martial. Lib. 1.
Vota tui breviter, &c.

WEll then, Sir, you shall know how far extend
  The Prayers and Hopes of your Poetick Friend;
He does not Palaces nor Manors crave,
Would be no Lord, but less a Lord would have.
The ground he holds, if he his own, can call,
He quarrels not with Heaven because 'tis small:
Let gay and toilsome Greatness others please,
He loves of homely Littleness the Ease.
Can any Man in guilded rooms attend,
And his dear houres in humble visits spend;
When in the fresh and beauteous Fields he may
With various healthful pleasures fill the day?
If there be Man (ye Gods) I ought to Hate
Dependance and Attendance be his Fate.
Still let him Busie be, and in a crowd,
And very much a Slave, and very Proud:
Thus he perhaps Pow'rful and Rich may grow;
No matter, O ye Gods! that I'le allow.
But let him Peace and Freedome never see;
Let him not love this Life, who loves not Me.

Martial. L. 2.
Vis fieri Liber? &c.

WOuld you be Free? 'Tis your chief wish, you say,
  Come on; I'le shew thee, Friend, the certain way,
If to no Feasts abroad thou lov'st to go,
Whilst bounteous God does Bread at home bestow,
If thou the goodness of thy Cloaths dost prize
By thine own Use, and not by others Eyes.

(If onely safe from Weathers) thou can'st dwell,
In a small House, but a convenient Shell,
If thou without a Sigh, or Golden wish,
Canst look upon thy Beechen Bowl, and Dish;
If in thy Mind such power and greatness be,
The *Persian* King's a Slave compar'd with Thee.

Mart. L. 2.

Quod te nomine? &c.

THat I do you with humble Bowes no more,
And danger of my naked Head adore.
That I who Lord and Master cry'd erewhile,
Salute you in a new and different Stile,
By your own Name, a scandal to you now,
Think not that I forget my self or you:
By loss of all things by all others sought
This Freedome, and the Freemans Hat is bought.
A Lord and Master no man wants but He
Who o're Himself has no Autoritie.
Who does for Honours and for Riches strive,
And Follies, without which Lords cannot Live.
If thou from Fortune dost no Servant crave,
Believe it, thou no Master need'st to have.

Ode.

Upon Liberty.

I.

FReedome with Virtue takes her seat,
Her proper place, her onely Scene,
Is in the Golden Mean,
She lives not with the Poor, nor with the Great.

The Wings of those Necessity has clipt,
         And they'r in Fortunes Bridewell whipt,
         To the laborious task of Bread;
These are by various Tyrants Captive lead.
Now wild Ambition with imperious force
Rides, raines, and spurs them like th' unruly Horse.
         And servile Avarice yoakes them now
         Like toilsome Oxen to the Plow.
And sometimes Lust, like the Misguiding Light,
Drawes them through all the Labyrinths of Night.
If any Few among the Great there be
         From these insulting Passions free,
         Yet we ev'n those too fetter'd see
By Custom, Business, Crowds, and formal Decency.
And whereso'ere they stay, and whereso'ere they go,
         Impertinencies round them flow:
         These are the small uneasie things
         Which about Greatness still are found,
         And rather it Molest then Wound:
Like Gnats which too much heat of summer brings;
But Cares do swarm there too, and those have stings:
As when the Honey does too open lie,
         A thousand Wasps about it fly:
Nor will the Master ev'n to share admit;
The Master stands aloof, and dares not Tast of it.

2.

'Tis Morning; well; I fain would yet sleep on;
         You cannot now; you must be gone
         To Court, or to the noisy Hall:
Besides, the Rooms without are crowded all;
         The stream of Business does begin,

And a Spring-Tide of Clients is come in.
Ah cruel Guards, which this poor Prisoner keep!
      Will they not suffer him to sleep?
Make an Escape; out at the Postern flee,
And get some blessed Houres of Libertie,
With a few Friends, and a few Dishes dine,
      And much of Mirth and moderate Wine.
To thy bent Mind some relaxation give,
And steal one day out of thy Life to Live.
Oh happy man (he cries) to whom kind Heaven
      Has such a Freedome alwayes given!
Why, mighty Madman, what should hinder thee
      From being every day as Free?

3.

In all the Freeborn Nations of the Air,
Never did Bird a spirit so mean and sordid bear,
As to exchange his Native Liberty
Of soaring boldly up into the sky,
His Liberty to Sing, to Perch, or Fly,
      When, and where'ver he thought good,
And all his innocent pleasures of the Wood,
For a more plentiful or constant Food.
      Nor ever did Ambitious rage
      Make him into a painted Cage;
Or the false Forest of a well-hung Room,
      For Honour and Preferment come.
Now, Blessings on ye all, ye Heroick Race,
Who keep their Primitive powers and rights so well
      Though Men and Angels fell.

Of all Material Lives the highest place,
      To you is justly given;
      And wayes and walkes the neerest Heaven.
Whilst wretched we, yet vain and proud, think fit
      To boast, That we look up to it.
Even to the Universal Tyrant Love,
      You Homage pay but once a year:
None so degenerous and unbirdly prove,
      As his perpetual yoke to bear.
None but a few unhappy Houshold Foul,
      Whom human Lordship does controul;
      Who from their birth corrupted were
By Bondage, and by mans Example here.

4.

He's no small Prince who every day
      Thus to himself can say,
Now will I sleep, now eat, now sit, now walk,
Now meditate alone, now with Acquaintance talk.
This I will do, here I will stay,
Or if my Fancy call me away,
My Man and I will presently go ride;
(For we before have nothing to provide,
Nor after are to render an account)
To *Dover*, *Barwick*, or the *Cornish* Mount.
      If thou but a short journey take,
      As if thy last thou wert to make,
Business must be dispatch'd e're thou canst part,
      Nor canst thou stirr unless there be
      A hundred Horse and Men to wait on thee,
      And many a Mule, and many a Cart;

What an unwieldy man thou art?
The *Rhodian Colossus* so
A Journey too might go.

5.

Where Honour or where Conscience does not bind
No other Law shall shackle me,
Slave to my self I will not be,
Nor shall my future Actions be confin'd
By my own present Mind.
Who by Resolves and Vows engag'd does stand
For days that yet belong to Fate,
Does like an unthrift Mortgage his Estate
Before it falls into his Hand,
The Bondman of the Cloister so
All that he does receive does always owe.
And still as Time comes in, it goes away
Not to Enjoy, but Debts to pay.
Unhappy Slave, and Pupil to a Bell!
Which his hours work as well as hours does tell!
Unhappy till the last, the kind releasing Knell.

6.

If Life should a well-order'd Poem be
(In which he only hits the white
Who joyns true Profit with the best Delight)
The more Heroique strain let others take,
Mine the Pindarique way I'le make.
The Matter shall be Grave, the Numbers loose and free.
It shall not keep one setled pace of Time,
In the same Tune it shall not always Chime,
Nor shall each day just to his Neighbour Rhime,

A thousand Liberties it shall dispense,
And yet shall mannage all without offence;
Or to the sweetness of the Sound, or greatness of the
    Sence,
Nor shall it never from one Subject start,
        Nor seek Transitions to depart,
Nor its set way o're Stiles and Bridges make,
        Nor thorough Lanes a Compass take
As if it fear'd some trespass to commit,
        When the wide Air's a Road for it.
So the Imperial Eagle does not stay
        Till the whole Carkass he devour
        That's fallen into its power.
As if his generous Hunger understood
That he can never want plenty of Food,
        He only sucks the tastful Blood.
And to fresh Game flies cheerfully away;
To Kites and meaner Birds he leaves the mangled Prey.

2. *Of Solitude.*

N *Unquam minus solus, quam cum solus,* is now become a very vulgar saying. Every Man and almost every Boy for these seventeen hundred years, has had it in his mouth. But it was at first spoken by the Excellent *Scipio,* who was without question a most Eloquent and Witty person, as well as the most Wise, most Worthy, most Happy, and the Greatest of all Mankind. His meaning no doubt was this, That he found more satisfaction to his mind, and more improvement of it by Solitude then by Company, and to shew that he spoke not this loosly or out of vanity, after he had made *Rome*, Mistriss of almost the whole World, he retired himself from it by a voluntary exile, and at a private house in the middle of a wood neer *Linternum*, passed the remainder of his Glorious life no less Gloriously. This House *Seneca* went to see so long after with great veneration, and among other things describes his Baths to have been of so mean a structure, that now, says he, the basest of the people would despise them, and cry out, poor *Scipio* under-stood not how to live. What an Authority is here for the credit of Retreat? and happy had it been for *Hannibal*, if Adversity could have taught him as much Wisdom as was learnt by *Scipio* from the highest prosperities. This would be no wonder if it were as truly as it is colourably and wittily said by Monsieur *de Montagne*. That Ambition it self might teach us to love Solitude; there's nothing does so much hate to have Companions. 'Tis true, it loves to have its Elbows free, it detests to have Company on either side, but it delights above all Things in a Train behind, I, and Ushers too before it. But the greatest part of men are so far from the opinion of that noble *Roman*, that if they chance at any time to be without company, they'r like a becalmed Ship, they never move but by the wind of other mens breath, and have no Oars of their own to steer withal. It is very fantastical and contradictory in humane Nature, that Men should love themselves above all the rest of the world, and yet never endure to be with themselves. When they are in love with a Mistriss, all other persons are importunate and burdensome to them. *Tecum vivere amem, tecum obeam Lubens*, They would live and dye with her alone.

> *Sic ego secretis possum benè vivere silvis*
> *Quà nulla humano sit via trita pedè,*
> *Tu mihi curarum requies, tu nocte vel atrâ*
> *Lumen, & in solis tu mihi turba locis.*

With thee for ever I in woods could rest,
Where never humane foot the ground has prest,
Thou from all shades the darkness canst exclude,
And from a Desart banish Solitude.

And yet our Dear Self is so wearisome to us, that we can scarcely support its conversation for an hour together. This is such an odd temper of mind as *Catullus* expresses towards one of his Mistresses, whom we may suppose to have been of a very unsociable humour.

> *Odi & Amo, quanám id faciam ratione requiris ?*
> *Nescio, sed fieri sentio, & excrucior.*

I Hate, and yet I Love thee too;
How can that be?   I know not how;
Only that so it is I know,
And feel with Torment that 'tis so.

It is a deplorable condition, this, and drives a man sometimes to pittiful shifts in seeking how to avoid Himself.

The truth of the matter is, that neither he who is a Fop in the world, is a fit man to be alone; nor he who has set his heart much upon the world, though he have never so much understanding; so that Solitude can be well fitted and set right, but upon a very few persons.

They must have enough knowledge of the World to see
the vanity of it, and enough Virtue to despise all
Vanity; if the Mind be possest with any Lust or
Passions, a man had better be in a Faire, then in a
Wood alone. They may like petty Thieves cheat us
perhaps, and pick our pockets in the midst of company,
but like Robbers they use to strip and bind, or murder
us when they catch us alone. This is but to retreat from
Men, and fall into the hands of Devils. 'Tis like the
punishment of Parricides among the *Romans*, to be
sow'd into a Bag with an Ape, a Dog, and a Serpent.
The first work therefore that a man must do to make
himself capable of the good of Solitude, is, the very
Eradication of all Lusts, for how is it possible for a Man
to enjoy himself while his Affections are tyed to things
without Himself? In the second place, he must learn
the Art and get the Habit of Thinking; for this too, no
less than well speaking, depends upon much practice,
and Cogitation is the thing which distinguishes the
Solitude of a God from a wild Beast. Now because
the soul of Man is not by its own Nature or observation furnisht with sufficient Materials to work upon;
it is necessary for it to have continual recourse to
Learning and Books for fresh supplies, so that the
solitary Life will grow indigent, and be ready to starve
without them; but if once we be throughly engaged
in the Love of Letters, instead of being wearied with
the length of any day, we shall only complain of the
shortness of our whole Life.

> *O vita, stulto longa, sapienti brevis !*
> O Life, long to the Fool, short to the Wise!

The first Minister of State has not so much business
in publique, as a wise man has in private; if the one
have little leasure to be alone, the other has less
leasure to be in company; the one has but part of the
affairs of one Nation, the other all the works of God
and Nature under his consideration. There is no saying
shocks me so much as that which I hear very often,
That a man does not know how to pass his Time.
'Twould have been but ill spoken by *Methusalem* in
the Nine hundred sixty ninth year of his Life, so far
it is from us, who have not time enough to attain to
the utmost perfection of any part of any Science, to
have cause to complain that we are forced to be idle
for want of work. But this you'l say is work only for
the Learned, others are nòt capable either of the employments or divertisements that arrive from Letters;
I know they are not; and therefore cannot much
recommend Solitude to a man totally illiterate. But
if any man be so unlearned as to want entertainment
of the little Intervals of accidental Solitude, which
frequently occurr in almost all conditions (except the
very meanest of the people, who have business enough
in the necessary provisions for Life) it is truly a great
shame both to his Parents and Himself, for a very
small portion of any Ingenious Art will stop up all
those gaps of our Time, either Musique, or Painting,
or Designing, or Chymistry, or History, or Gardening,
or twenty other things will do it usefully and pleasantly;
and if he happen to set his affections upon Poetry
(which I do not advise him too immoderately) that
will over do it; no wood will be thick enough to hide

him from the importunities of company or business,
which would abstract him from his Beloved.

——O quis me gelidis sub montibus Æmi
Sistat, & ingenti ramorum protegat umbrâ?

1.

Hail, old *Patrician* Trees, so great and good!
    Hail ye *Plebeian* under wood!
    Where the Poetique Birds rejoyce,
And for their quiet Nests and plentious Food,
    Pay with their grateful voice.

2.

Hail, the poor Muses richest Mannor Seat!
    Ye Countrey Houses and Retreat,
    Which all the happy Gods so Love,
That for you oft they quit their Bright and Great
    Metropolis above.

3.

Here Nature does a House for me erect,
    Nature the wisest Architect,
    Who those fond Artists does despise
That can the fair and living Trees neglect;
    Yet the Dead Timber prize.

4.

Here let me careless and unthoughtful lying,
    Hear the soft winds above me flying,
    With all their wanton Boughs dispute,
And the more tuneful Birds to both replying
    Nor be my self too Mute.

5.

A Silver stream shall roul his waters neer,
  Guilt with the Sun-beams here and there
  On whose enamel'd Bank I'll walk,
And see how prettily they Smile, and hear
  How prettily they Talk.

6.

Ah wretched, and too Solitary Hee
  Who loves not his own Company!
  He'l feel the weight of't many a day
Unless he call in Sin or Vanity
  To help to bear't away.

7.

Oh Solitude, first state of Human-kind!
  Which blest remain'd till man did find
  Even his own helpers Company.
As soon as two (alas!) together joyn'd,
  The Serpent made up Three.

8.

Though God himself, through countless Ages Thee
  His sole Companion chose to be,
  Thee, Sacred Solitude alone,
Before the Branchy head of Numbers Tree
  Sprang from the Trunk of One.

9.

Thou (though men think thine an unactive part)
  Dost break and tame th'unruly heart,
  Which else would know no setled pace,
Making it move, well mannag'd by thy Art,
  With Swiftness and with Grace.

10.

Thou the faint beams of Reasons scatter'd Light,
        Dost like a Burning-glass unite,
        Dost multiply the feeble Heat,
And fortifie the strength, till thou dost bright
        And noble Fires beget.

11.

Whilst this hard Truth I teach, methinks, I see
        The Monster *London* laugh at me,
        I should at thee too, foolish City,
If it were fit to laugh at Misery,
        But thy Estate I pity.

12.

Let but thy wicked men from out thee go,
        And all the Fools that crowd thee so,
        Even thou who dost thy Millions boast,
A Village less then *Islington* wilt grow,
        A Solitude almost.

3. *Of Obscurity.*

N *AM neque Divitibus contingunt gaudia solis,*
        Nec vixit male, qui natus moriensque Fefellit.

God made not pleasures only for the Rich,
Nor have those men without their share too liv'd,
Who both in Life and Death the world deceiv'd.

This seems a strange Sentence thus literally translated,
and looks as if it were in vindication of the men of
business (for who else can Deceive the world?) whereas

it is in commendation of those who live and dye so
obscurely, that the world takes no notice of them.
This *Horace* calls deceiving the world, and in another
place uses the same phrase.

> *Secretum iter & Fallentis semita vitæ.*
> *The secret tracks of the Deceiving Life.*

It is very elegant in Latine, but our English word
will hardly bear up to that sence, and therefore
Mr. *Broom* translates it very well,

> *Or from a Life, led as it were by stealth.*

Yet we say in our Language, a thing deceives our sight,
when it passes before us unperceived, and we may say
well enough out of the same Authour,

> *Sometimes with sleep, somtimes with wine we strive,*
> *The cares of Life and troubles to Deceive.*

But that is not to deceive the world, but to deceive
our selves, as *Quintilian* saies, *Vitam fallere*, To d raw
on still, and amuse, and deceive our Life, till it be
advanced insensibly to the fatal Period, and fall into
that Pit which Nature hath prepared for it. The
meaning of all this is no more then that most vulgar
saying, *Bene qui latuit, bene vixit,* He has lived well,
who has lain well hidden. Which if it be a truth, the
world (I'le swear) is sufficiently deceived: For my part,
I think it is, and that the pleasantest condition of Life,
is *in Incognito*. What a brave Privilege is it to be free
from all Contentions, from all Envying or being
Envyed, from recieving and from paying all kind of
Ceremonies? It is in my mind, a very delightful
pastime, for two good and agreeable friends to travail

up and down together, in places where they are by
no body known, nor know any body. It was the case
of *Æneas* and his *Achates*, when they walkt invisibly
about the fields and streets of *Carthage*, *Venus* her self

> *A vail of thickned Air around them cast,*
> *That none might know, or see them as they past.*

The common story of *Demosthenes's* confession that he
had taken great pleasure in hearing of a Tanker-
woman say as he past; This is that *Demosthenes*, is
wonderful ridiculous from so solid an Orator. I my
self have often met with that temptation to vanity
(if it were any) but am so far from finding it any
pleasure, that it only makes me run faster from the
place, till I get, as it were out of sight-shot. *Democritus*
relates, and in such a manner, as if he gloried in the
good fortune and commodity of it, that when he came
to *Athens* no body there did so much as take notice
of him; and *Epicurus* lived there very well, that is,
Lay hid many years in his Gardens, so famous since
that time, with his friend *Metrodorus*: after whose
death, making in one of his letters a kind commemoration of the happiness which they two had injoyed
together, he adds at last, that he thought it no disparagement to those great felicities of their life, that
in the midst of the most talk'd-of and Talking Country
in the world, they had lived so long, not only without
Fame, but almost without being heard of. And yet
within a very few years afterward, there were no two
Names of men more known or more generally celebrated. If we engage into a large Acquaintance and

various familiarities, we set open our gates to the
Invaders of most of our time: we expose our life to a
Quotidian Ague of frigid impertinencies, which would
make a wise man tremble to think of. Now, as for
being known much by sight, and pointed at, I cannot
comprehend the honour that lies in that: Whatsoever
it be, every Mountebank has it more then the best
Doctor, and the Hangman more then the Lord Chief
Justice of a City. Every creature has it both of Nature
and Art if it be any ways extraordinary. It was as
often said, This is that *Bucephalus*, or, This is that
Incitatus, when they were led prancing through the
streets, as, this is that *Alexander*, or this is that
Domitian; and truly for the latter, I take *Incitatus* to
have bin a much more Honourable Beast then his
Master, and more deserving the Consulship, then he
the Empire. I love and commend a true good Fame,
because it is the shadow of Virtue, not that it doth
any good to the Body which it accompanies, but 'tis
an efficacious shadow, and like that of St. *Peter* cures
the Diseases of others. The best kinde of Glory, no
doubt, is that which is reflected from Honesty, such
as was the Glory of *Cato* and *Aristides*, but it was
harmful to them both, and is seldom beneficial to any
man whilst he lives, what it is to him after his death,
I cannot say, because, I love not *Philosophy* merely
notional and conjectural, and no man who has made
the Experiment has been so kind as to come back to
inform us. Upon the whole matter, I account a person
who has a moderate Minde and Fortune, and lives in
the conversation of two or three agreeable friends, with

little commerce in the world besides, who is esteemed well enough by his few neighbours that know him, and is truly irreproachable by any body, and so after a healthful quiet life, before the great inconveniences of old age, goes more silently out of it then he came in, (for I would not have him so much as Cry in the *Exit*). This Innocent Deceiver of the world, as *Horace* calls him, this *Muta persona*, I take to have been more happy in his Part, then the greatest Actors that fill the Stage with show and noise, nay, even then *Augustus* himself, who askt with his last breath, Whether he had not played his *Farce* very well.

Seneca, ex Thyeste,

Act. 2. Chor.

Stet quicunque volet, potens
Aulæ culmine lubrico, &c.

Upon the slippery tops of humane State,
    The guilded Pinnacles of Fate,
Let others proudly stand, and for a while
    The giddy danger to beguile,
With Joy, and with disdain look down on all,
    Till their Heads turn, and down they fall.
Me, O ye Gods, on Earth, or else so near
    That I no Fall to Earth may fear,
And, O ye gods, at a good distance seat
    From the long Ruines of the Great.
Here wrapt in th' Arms of Quiet let me ly;
Quiet, Companion of Obscurity.
Here let my Life, with as much silence slide,
    As Time that measures it does glide.

Nor let the Breath of Infamy or Fame,
From town to town Eccho about my Name.
Nor let my homely Death embroidered be
        With Scutcheon or with Elegie.
        An old *Plebean* let me Dy,
Alas, all then are such as well as I.
        To him, alas, to him, I fear,
The face of Death will terrible appear:
Who in his life flattering his senceless pride
By being known to all the world beside,
Does not himself, when he is Dying know
Nor what he is, nor Whither hee's to go.

4. *Of Agriculture.*

THE first wish of *Virgil* (as you will find anon by his Verses) was to be a good Philosopher; the second, a good Husbandman; and God (whom he seem'd to understand better then most of the most learned Heathens) dealt with him just as he did with *Solomon*; because he prayed for wisdom in the first place, he added all things else which were subordinately to be desir'd. He made him one of the best Philosophers, and best Husbandmen, and to adorn and communicate both those faculties, the best Poet: He made him besides all this a rich man, and a man who desired to be no richer. *O Fortunatus nimium, & bona qui sua novit:* To be a Husbandman, is but a retreat from the City; to be a Philosopher, from the world, or rather, a Retreat from the world, as it is mans; into the world, as it is Gods. But since Nature denies to most men the capacity or appetite, and Fortune allows but to a very few the opportunities or possibility of applying themselves wholy to Philosophy, the best mixture of humane affairs that we can make, are the employments of a Country life. It is, as *Columella* calls it, *Res sine dubitatione proxima, & quasi Consanguinea Sapientiæ*, The nearest Neighbour, or rather next in Kindred to Philosophy. *Varro* sayes, the Principles of it are the same which *Ennius* made to be the Principles of all Nature: Earth, Water, Air, and the Sun. It does certainly comprehend more parts of Philosophy then any one Profession, Art or Science in the world besides: and therefore *Cicero* saies, The pleasures of a Husbandman, *Mihi ad sapientis vitam proxime videntur accedere*, Come very nigh to those of a Philosopher. There is no other sort of life that affords so many branches of praise to a Panegyrist: The Utility of it to a mans self: The Usefulness, or rather Necessity of it to all the rest of Mankind: The Innocence, the Pleasure, the Antiquity, the Dignity. The Utility (I mean plainly the Lucre of it) is not so great now in our Nation as arises from Merchandise and the trading of the City, from whence many of the best Estates and chief Honours of the Kingdom are derived: we have no men now fetcht from the Plow to be made Lords, as they were in *Rome* to be made Consuls and Dictators, the reason of which I conceive to be from an evil Custom, now grown as strong among us, as if it were a Law, which is, that no men put their Children to be bred up Apprentices in Agriculture, as in other Trades, but such who are so poor, that when they come to be men, they have not wherewithall to

set up in it, and so can only Farm some small parcel
of ground, the Rent of which devours all but the bare
Subsistence of the Tenant: Whilst they who are
Proprietors of the Land, are either too proud, or, for
want of that kind of Education, too ignorant to im-
prove their Estates, though the means of doing it be
as easie and certain in this as in any other track of
Commerce: If there were alwaies two or three thousand
youths, for seven or eight years bound to this Profession, that they might learn the whole Art of it, and
afterwards be enabled to be Masters in it, by a
moderate stock: I cannot doubt but that we should
see as many Aldermens Estates made in the Country,
as now we do out of all kind of Merchandizing in the
City. There are as many wayes to be Rich, and which
is better, there is no Possibility to be poor, without
such negligence as can neither have excuse nor Pity;
for a little ground will without question feed a little
family, and the superfluities of Life (which are now
in some cases by custome made almost necessary)
must be supplyed out of the superabundance of Art
and Industry, or contemned by as great a Degree of
Philosophy. As for the Necessity of this Art, it is
evident enough, since this can live without all others,
and no one other without this. This is like Speech,
without which the Society of men cannot be preserved;
the others like Figures and Tropes of Speech which
serve only to adorn it. Many Nations have lived, and
some do still, without any Art but this; not so Ele-
gantly, I confess, but still they Live, and almost all
the other Arts which are here practised, are beholding

to this for most of their Materials. The Innocence of
this Life is the next thing for which I commend it,
and if Husbandmen preserve not that, they are much
to blame, for no men are so free from the Tempta-
tions of Iniquity. They live by what they can get by
Industry from the Earth, and others by what they
can catch by Craft from men. They live upon an
Estate given them by their Mother, and others upon
an Estate cheated from their Brethren. They live
like Sheep and Kine, by the allowances of Nature,
and others like Wolves and Foxes by the acquisi-
tions of Rapine. And, I hope, I may affirm (without any offence to the Great) that Sheep and Kine
are very useful, and that Wolves and Foxes are
pernicious creatures. They are without dispute of all
men the most quiet and least apt to be inflamed to
the disturbance of the Common-wealth: their manner
of Life inclines them, and Interest binds them to love
Peace: In our late mad and miserable Civil Wars, all
other Trades, even to the meanest, set forth whole
Troopes, and raised up some great Commanders, who
became famous and mighty for the mischiefs they had
done: But, I do not remember the Name of any one
Husbandman who had so considerable a share in the
twenty years ruine of his Country, as to deserve the
Curses of his Country-men: And if great delights be
joyn'd with so much Innocence, I think it is ill done
of men not to take them here where they are so tame,
and ready at hand, rather then hunt for them in
Courts and Cities, where they are so wild, and the
chase so troublesome and dangerous.

We are here among the vast and noble Scenes of
Nature; we are there among the pitiful shifts of Policy:
We walk here in the light and open wayes of the Divine
Bounty; we grope there in the dark and confused
Labyrinths of Human Malice: Our Senses are here
feasted with the clear and genuine taste of their
Objects, which are all Sophisticated there, and for
the most part overwhelmed with their contraries. Here
Pleasure looks (methinks) like a beautiful, constant,
and modest Wife; it is there an impudent, fickle, and
painted Harlot. Here is harmless and cheap Plenty,
there guilty and expenseful Luxury.

I shall onely instance in one Delight more, the most
natural and best natur'd of all others, a perpetual
companion of the Husbandman; and that is, the satisfaction of looking round about him, and seeing nothing
but the effects and improvements of his own Art and
Diligence; to be alwayes gathering of some Fruits of
it, and at the same time to behold others ripening, and
others budding: to see all his Fields and Gardens
covered with the beauteous Creatures of his own Industry; and to see, like God, that all his works are Good.

> ——*Hinc atque hinc glomerantur Oreades; ipsi.*
> *Agricolæ tacitum pertentant gaudia pectus.*

On his heart-strings a secret Joy does strike.

The Antiquity of his Art is certainly not to be con-
tested by any other. The three first Men in the World,
were a Gardner, a Ploughman, and a Grazier; and if
any man object, That the second of these was a
Murtherer, I desire he would consider, that as soon

as he was so, he quitted our Profession, and turn'd
Builder. It is for this reason, I suppose, that *Ecclesi-
asticus* forbids us to hate Husbandry; because (sayes
he) the most High has created it. We were all Born
to this Art, and taught by Nature to nourish our
Bodies by the same Earth out of which they were
made, and to which they must return, and pay at last
for their sustenance.

Behold the Original and Primitive Nobility of all
those great Persons, who are too proud now, not onely
to till the Ground, but almost to tread upon it. We
may talke what we please of Lilies, and Lions Rampant,
and Spread-Eagles in Fields d'Or, or d'Argent; but if
Heraldry were guided by Reason, a Plough in a Field
Arable, would be the most Noble and Antient Armes.

All these considerations make me fall into the wonder
and complaint of *Columella*, How it should come to
pass that all Arts or Sciences, (for the dispute, which
is an Art, and which a Science, does not belong to
the curiosity of us Husbandmen) *Metaphysick, Physick,
Morality, Mathematicks, Logick, Rhetorick*, &c. which
are all, I grant, good and usefull faculties, (except onely
Metaphysick which I do not know whether it be any
thing or no) but even *Vaulting, Fencing, Dancing,
Attiring, Cookery, Carving*, and such like Vanities,
should all have publick Schools and Masters; and yet
that we should never see or hear of any man who took
upon him the Profession of teaching this so pleasant, so
virtuous, so profitable, so honourable, so necessary Art.

A man would think, when he's in serious humour,
that it were but a vain, irrational and ridiculous thing,

for a great company of Men and Women to run up
and down in a Room together, in a hundred several
postures and figures, to no purpose, and with no design;
and therefore Dancing was invented first, and onely
practised anciently in the Ceremonies of the Heathen
Religion, which consisted all in Mommery and Madness; the latter being the chief glory of the Worship,
and accounted Divine Inspiration: This, I say, a severe
Man would think, though I dare not determine so far
against so customary a part now of good breeding. And
yet, who is there among our Gentry, that does not
entertain a Dancing Master for his Children as soon
as they are able to walk? But, Did ever any Father
provide a Tutor for his Son to instruct him betimes
in the Nature and Improvements of that Land which
he intended to leave him? That is at least a superfluity,
and this a Defect in our manner of Education; and
therefore I could wish (but cannot in these times much
hope to see it) that one Colledge in each University were
erected, and appropriated to this study, as well as
there are to Medecin, and the Civil Law: There would
be no need of making a Body of Scholars and Fellowes,
with certain endowments, as in other Colledges; it would
suffice, if after the manner of Halls in *Oxford*, there were
only four Professors constituted (for it would be too
much work for onely one Master, or Principal, as they
call him there) to teach these four parts of it. First,
Aration, and all things relating to it. Secondly, *Pastur-
age*. Thirdly, *Gardens, Orchards, Vineyards* and *Woods*.
Fourthly, All parts of *Rural Oeconomy*, which would
contain the Government of *Bees, Swine, Poultry, Decoys,*

Ponds, &c. and all that which *Varro* calls *Villaticas Pastiones*, together with the Sports of the Field (which ought to be looked upon not onely as Pleasures, but as parts of House-keeping) and the Domestical conservation and uses of all that is brought in by Industry abroad. The business of these Professors should not be, as is commonly practised in other Arts, onely to read Pompous and Superficial Lectures out of *Virgils Georgickes*, *Pliny*, *Varro* or *Columella*, but to instruct their Pupils in the whole Method and course of this study, which might be run through perhaps with diligence in a year or two; and the continual succession of Scholars upon a moderate taxation for their Diet, Lodging, and Learning, would be a sufficient constant revenue for Maintenance of the House and the Professors, who should be men not chosen for the Ostentation of Critical Literature, but for solid and experimental Knowledge of the things they teach such Men; so industrious and publick-spirited as I conceive Mr. *Hartlib* to be, if the Gentleman be yet alive: But it is needless to speak farther of my thoughts of this Design, unless the present Disposition of the Age allowed more probability of bringing it into execution. What I have further to say of the Country Life, shall be borrowed from the Poets, who were alwayes the most faithful and affectionate friends to it. Poetry was Born among the Shepherds.

> *Nescio qua Natale solum dulcedine Musas*
> *Ducit, & immemores non sinit esse sui.*

The Muses still love their own Native place,
T'has secret Charms which nothing can deface.

The truth is, no other place is proper for their work; one might as well undertake to Dance in a Crowd, as to make good Verses in the midst of Noise and Tumult.

As well might Corn as Verse in Cities grow;
In vain the thankless Glebe we Plow and Sow,
Against th' unnatural Soil in vain we strive;
'Tis not a Ground in which these Plants will thrive.

It will bear nothing but the Nettles or Thornes of *Satyre*, which grow most naturally in the worst Earth; And therefore almost all Poets, except those who were not able to eat Bread without the bounty of Great men, that is, without what they could get by Flattering of them, have not onely withdrawn themselves from the Vices and Vanities of the Grand World (*Pariter vitiisque Jocisque Altius humanis exeruere caput*) into the innocent happiness of a retired Life; but have commended and adorned nothing so much by their Ever-living Poems. *Hesiod* was the first or second Poet in the World that remaines yet extant (if *Homer*, as some think, preceded him, but I rather believe they were Contemporaries) and he is the first Writer too of the Art of Husbandry: He has contributed (sayes *Columella*) not a little to our Profession; I suppose he means not a little Honour, for the matter of his Instructions is not very important: His great Antiquity is visible through the Gravity and Simplicity of his Stile. The most Acute of all his sayings concerns our purpose very much, and is couched in the reverend obscurity of an Oracle. Πλέον ἥμισυ Παντός. The half is more then the whole. The occasion of the speech is this; His Brother *Perses* had by corrupting some great men (Βασιλῆας Δωροφάγους, Great Bribe-eaters he calls them) gotten from him the half of his Estate. It is no Matter, (says he) they have not done me so much prejudice, as they imagine.

Νήπιοι, οὐδ᾽ ἴσασιν ὅσῳ Πλέον Ἥμισυ Παντός,
Οὐδ᾽ ὅσον ἐν μαλάχῃ τε καὶ ἀσφοδέλῳ μέγ᾽ ὄνειαρ,
Κρύψαντες γὰρ ἔχουσι θεοὶ βίον ἀνθρώποισι.

Unhappy they to whom God has not reveal'd
By a strong Light which must their sence controle,
That halfe a great Estate's more then the whole:
Unhappy, from whom still conceal'd does lie
Of Roots and Herbs, the wholesome Luxurie.

This I conceive to have been Honest *Hesiods* meaning. From *Homer* we must not expect much concerning our affairs. He was Blind and could neither work in the Countrey, nor enjoy the pleasures of it, his helpless Poverty was likeliest to be sustained in the richest places, he was to delight the *Grecians* with fine tales of the Wars and adventures of their Ancestors; his Subject removed him from all Commerce with us, and yet, methinks, he made a shift to show his good will a little. For though he could do us no Honour in the person of his *Hero Ulisses* (much less of *Achilles*) because his whole time was consumed in Wars and Voyages, yet he makes his Father *Laertes* a Gardener all that while, and seeking his Consolation for the absence of his son in the pleasure of Planting and even Dunging his own grounds. Ye see he did not contemn us Peasants, nay, so far was he from that insolence,

that he always stiles *Eumæus*, who kept the Hogs with
wonderful respect Δῖον ὑφορβόν. The Divine Swine-
herd he could ha' done no more for *Menelaus* or *Agamem-
non*. And *Theocritus* (a very ancient Poet, but he was one
of our own Tribe, for he wrote nothing but Pastorals)
gave the same Epithete to an Husbandman 'Αμείβετο
Δῖος ἀγρώτης. The Divine Husbandman replyed to
Hercules, who was but Δῖος Himself. These were Civil
Greeks! and who understood the Dignity of our
Calling! among the *Romans* we have in the first place,
our truly Divine *Virgil*, who, though by the favour of
Mæcenas and *Augustus*, he might have been one of
the chief men of *Rome*, yet chose rather to employ
much of his time in the exercise, and much of his immortal wit in the praise and instructions of a Rustique
Life, who though he had written before whole Books
of Pastorals and *Georgiques* could not abstain in his
great and Imperial Poem from describing *Evander*, one
of his best Princes, as living just after the homely
manner of an ordinary Countreyman. He seats him
in a Throne of Maple, and lays him but upon a Bears
skin, the Kine and Oxen are lowing in his Court yard,
the Birds under the Eeves of his Window call him up
in the morning, and when he goes abroad, only two
Dogs go along with him for his guard: at last when he
brings *Æneas* into his Royal Cottage, he makes him
say this memorable complement, greater then ever
yet was spoken at the *Escurial*, the *Louvre*, or our
Whitehall.

———— *Hæc (inquit) limina victor*
Alcides subiit, hæc illum Regia cepit,

*Aude, Hospes, contemnere opes, & te quoque dignum
Finge Deo, rebusque veni non asper egenis.*

This humble Roof, this rustique Court (said He)
Receiv'd *Alcides* crown'd with victory.
Scorn not (Great Guest) the steps where he has trod,
But contemn Wealth, and imitate a God.

The next Man whom we are much obliged to, both
for his Doctrine and Example, is the next best Poet
in the world to *Virgil*; his dear friend *Horace*, who
when *Augustus* had desired *Mæcenas* to perswade him
to come and live domestically, and at the same Table
with him, and to be Secretary of State of the whole
World under him, or rather joyntly with him, for he
says, *ut nos in Epistolis scribendis adjuvet*, could not
be tempted to forsake his *Sabin*, or *Tiburtin* Mannor,
for so rich and so glorious a trouble. There was never,
I think, such an example as this in the world, that he
should have so much moderation and courage as to
refuse an offer of such greatness, and the Emperour
so much generosity and good Nature as not to be at
all offended with his refusal, but to retain still the
same kindness, and express it often to him in most
friendly and familiar Letters, part of which are still
extant. If I should produce all the passages of this
excellent Author upon the several Subjects which I
treat of in this Book, I must be obliged to translate
half his works; of which I may say more truly than
in my opinion he did of *Homer, Qui quid sit pulchrum,
quid Turpe, quid utile, quid non, plenius & melius
Chrysippo, & Crantore dicit.* I shall content my self

upon this particular Theme with three only, one out
of his *Odes*, the other out of his *Satyrs*, the third out
of his *Epistles*, and shall forbear to collect the suffrages
of all other Poets, which may be found scattered up
and down through all their writings, and especially
in *Martials*. But I must not omit to make some
excuse for the bold undertaking of my own unskilful
Pencil upon the beauties of a Face that has been
drawn before by so many great Masters, especially,
that I should dare to do it in *Latine* verses (though of
another kind) and have the confidence to Translate
them. I can only say that I love the Matter, and that
ought to cover many faults; and that I run not to
contend with those before me, but follow to applaud
them.

Virg. Georg.

O fortunatos nimium, &c.

A Translation out of *Virgil*.

OH happy, (if his Happiness he knows)
　　The Country Swain, on whom kind Heav'n bestows
At home all Riches that wise Nature needs;
Whom the just earth with easie plenty feeds.
'Tis true, no morning Tide of Clients comes,
And fills the painted Chanels of his rooms,
Adoring the rich Figures, as they pass,
In Tap'stry wrought, or cut in living brass;
Nor is his Wooll superfluously dy'd
With the dear Poyson of *Assyrian* pride:
Nor do *Arabian* Perfumes vainly spoil
The Native Use, and Sweetness of his Oyl.

Instead of these, his calm and harmless life
Free from th' Alarms of Fear, and storms of Strife,
Does with substantial blessedness abound,
And the soft wings of Peace cover him round:
Through artless Grots the murmuring waters glide;
Thick Trees both against Heat and Cold provide,
From whence the Birds salute him; and his ground
With lowing Herds, and bleeting Sheep does sound;
And all the Rivers, and the Forests nigh,
Both Food and Game, and Exercise supply.
Here a well hard'ned active youth we see,
Taught the great Art of chearful Poverty.
Here, in this place alone, there still do shine
Some streaks of Love, both humane and Divine;
From hence *Astræa* took her flight, and here
Still her last Foot-steps upon Earth appear.
'Tis true, the first desire which does controul
All the inferiour wheels that move my Soul,
Is, that the Muse me her high Priest would make;
Into her holyest Scenes of Myst'ry take,
And open there to my mind's purged eye
Those wonders which to Sense the Gods deny;
How in the Moon such change of shapes is found:
The Moon, the changing Worlds eternal bound.
What shakes the solid Earth, what strong disease
Dares trouble the firm Centre's antient ease;
What makes the Sea retreat, and what advance:
Varieties too regular for chance.
What drives the Chariot on of Winters light,
And stops the lazy Waggon of the night.
But if my dull and frozen Blood deny,

To send forth Sp'rits that raise a Soul so high;
In the next place, let Woods and Rivers be
My quiet, though unglorious destiny.
In Life's cool vale let my low Scene be laid;
Cover me Gods, with *Tempe's* thickest shade.
Happy the Man, I grant, thrice happy he
Who can through gross effects their causes see:
Whose courage from the deeps of knowledg springs,
Nor vainly fears inevitable things;
But does his walk of virtue calmly go,
Through all th' allarms of Death and Hell below.
Happy! but next such Conquerours, happy they,
Whose humble Life lies not in fortunes way.
They unconcern'd from their safe distant seat,
Behold the Rods and Scepters of the great.
The quarrels of the mighty without fear,
And the descent of forein Troops they hear.
Nor can even *Rome* their steddy course misguide,
With all the lustre of her perishing Pride.
Them never yet did strife or avarice draw,
Into the noisy markets of the Law,
The Camps of Gowned War, nor do they live
By rules or forms that many mad men give.
Duty for Natures Bounty they repay,
And her sole Laws religiously obey.

   Some with bold Labour plow the faithless main,
Some rougher storms in Princes Courts sustain.
Some swell up their sleight sails with pop'ular fame,
Charm'd with the foolish whistlings of a Name.
Some their vain wealth to Earth again commit;
With endless cares some brooding o're it sit.

Country and Friends are by some Wretches sold,
To lie on *Tyrian* Beds and drink in Gold;
No price too high for profit can be shown;
Not Brothers blood, nor hazards of their own.
Around the World in search of it they roam,
It makes ev'n their Antipodes their home;
Mean while, the prudent Husbandman is found,
In mutual duties striving with his ground,
And half the year he care of that does take,
That half the year grateful returns does make.
Each fertil moneth does some new gifts present,
And with new work his industry content.
This, the young Lamb, that the soft Fleece doth yield,
This, loads with Hay, and that, with Corn the Field:
All sorts of Fruit crown the rich *Autumns* Pride:
And on a swelling Hill's warm stony side,
The powerful Princely Purple of the Vine,
Twice dy'd with the redoubled Sun, does shine.
In th' Evening to a fair ensuing day,
With joy he sees his Flocks and Kids to play;
And loaded Kyne about his Cottage stand,
Inviting with known sound the Milkers hand;
And when from wholsom labour he doth come,
With wishes to be there, and wish't for home,
He meets at door the softest humane blisses,
His chast Wives welcom, and dear Childrens kisses.
When any Rural Holy dayes invite
His Genius forth to innocent delight,
On Earth's fair bed beneath some sacred shade,
Amidst his equal friends carelesly laid,
He sings thee *Bacchus* Patron of the Vine,

The Beechen Boul fomes with a floud of Wine,
Not to the loss of reason or of strength:
To active games and manly sport at length,
Their mirth ascends, and with fill'd veins they see,
Who can the best at better trials be.
Such was the Life the prudent *Sabins* chose,
From such the old *Hetrurian* virtue rose.
Such, *Remus* and the God his Brother led,
From such firm footing *Rome* grew the World's head.
Such was the Life that ev'n till now does raise
The honour of poor *Saturns* golden dayes:
Before Men born of Earth and buried there,
Let in the Sea their mortal fate to share.
Before new wayes of perishing were sought,
Before unskilful Death on Anvils wrought.
Before those Beasts which humane Life sustain,
By Men, unless to the Gods use were slain.

Horat. Epodon.

Beatus ille qui procul, &c.

HAppy the Man whom bounteous Gods allow
With his own Hands Paternal Grounds to plough!
Like the first golden Mortals Happy he
From Business and the cares of Money free!
No humane storms break off at Land his sleep.
No loud Alarms of Nature on the Deep,
From all the cheats of Law he lives secure,
Nor does th' affronts of Palaces endure;
Sometimes the beauteous Marriagable Vine
He to the lusty Bridegroom Elm does joyn;

Sometimes he lops the barren Trees around,
And grafts new Life into the fruitful wound;
Sometimes he sheers his Flock, and sometimes he
Stores up the Golden Treasures of the Bee.
He sees his lowing Herds walk o're the Plain,
Whilst neighbouring Hills low back to them again:
And when the Season Rich as well as Gay,
All her Autumnal Bounty does display.
How is he pleas'd th' encreasing Use to see,
Of his well trusted Labours bend the tree?
Of which large shares, on the glad sacred daies
He gives to Friends, and to the Gods repays.
With how much joy do's he beneath some shade
By aged trees rev'rend embraces made,
His careless head on the fresh Green recline,
His head uncharg'd with Fear or with Design.
By him a River constantly complaines,
The Birds above rejoyce with various strains
And in the solemn Scene their *Orgies* keep
Like Dreams mixt with the Gravity of sleep,
Sleep which does alwaies there for entrance wait
And nought within against it shuts the gate.
  Nor does the roughest season of the sky,
Or sullen *Jove* all sports to him deny,
He runs the *Mazes* of the nimble Hare,
His well-mouth'd Dogs glad concert rends the air,
Or with game bolder, and rewarded more,
He drives into a Toil, the foaming Bore,
Here flies the Hawk t' assault, and there the Net
To intercept the travailing foul is set.
And all his malice, all his craft is shown

In innocent wars, on beasts and birds alone.
This is the life from all misfortunes free,
From thee the Great one, Tyrant Love, from Thee;
And if a chaste and clean, though homely wife
Be added to the blessings of this Life,
Such as the antient Sun-burnt *Sabins* were,
Such as *Apulia*, frugal still, does bear,
Who makes her Children and the house her care,
And joyfully the work of Life does share,
Nor thinks herself too noble or too fine
To pin the sheepfold or to milch the Kine,
Who waits at door against her Husband come
From rural duties, late, and wearied home,
Where she receives him with a kind embrace,
A chearful Fire, and a more chearful Face:
And fills the Boul up to her homely Lord,
And with domestique plenty loads the board.
Not all the lustful shel-fish of the Sea,
Drest by the wanton hand of Luxurie,
Nor *Ortalans* nor *Godwits* nor the rest
Of costly names that glorify a Feast,
Are at the Princely tables better cheer,
Then Lamb and Kid, Lettice and Olives here.

The Country Mouse.

A Paraphrase upon Horace 2 *Book*, Satyr. 6.

AT the large foot of a fair hollow tree,
Close to plow'd ground, seated commodiously,
His antient and Hereditary House,
There dwelt a good substantial Country-Mouse:

4—2

Frugal, and grave, and careful of the main,
Yet, one, who once did nobly entertain
A City Mouse well coated, sleek, and gay,
A Mouse of high degree, which lost his way,
Wantonly walking forth to take the Air,
And arriv'd early, and belighted there,
For a days lodging: the good hearty Hoast,
(The antient plenty of his hall to boast)
Did all the stores produce, that might excite,
With various tasts, the Courtiers appetite.
Fitches and Beans, Peason, and Oats, and Wheat,
And a large Chesnut, the delicious meat
Which *Jove* himself, were he a Mouse, would eat.
And for a *Haut goust* there was mixt with these
The swerd of Bacon, and the coat of Cheese.
The precious Reliques, which at Harvest, he
Had gather'd from the Reapers luxurie.
Freely (said he) fall on and never spare,
The bounteous Gods will for to morrow care.
And thus at ease on beds of straw they lay,
And to their Genius sacrific'd the day.
Yet the nice guest's Epicurean mind,
(Though breeding made him civil seem and kind)
Despis'd this Country feast, and still his thought
Upon the Cakes and Pies of *London* wrought.
Your bounty and civility (said he)
Which I'm surpriz'd in these rude parts to see,
Shews that the Gods have given you a mind,
Too noble for the fate which here you find.
Why should a Soul, so virtuous and so great,
Lose it self thus in an Obscure retreat?

Let savage Beasts lodg in a Country Den,
You should see Towns, and Manners know, and men:
And taste the generous Lux'ury of the Court,
Where all the Mice of quality resort;
Where thousand beauteous shees about you move,
And by high fare, are plyant made to love.
We all e're long must render up our breath,
No cave or hole can shelter us from death.

   Since Life is so uncertain, and so short,
Let's spend it all in feasting and in sport.
Come, worthy Sir, come with me, and partake,
All the great things that mortals happy make.

   Alas, what virtue hath sufficient Arms,
T'oppose bright Honour, and soft Pleasures charms?
What wisdom can their magick force repel?
It draws this reverend Hermit from his Cel.
It was the time, when witty Poets tell,
That Phœbus *into* Thetis *bosom fell:*
She blusht at first, and then put out the light,
And drew the modest Curtains of the night.
Plainly, the troth to tell, the Sun was set,
When to the Town our wearied Travellers get,
To a Lords house, as Lordly as can be
Made for the use of Pride and Luxury,
They come; the gentle Courtier at the door
Stops and will hardly enter in before.
But 'tis, Sir, your command, and being so,
I'm sworn t' obedience, and so in they go.
Behind a hanging in a spacious room,
(The richest work of *Mortclakes* noble Loom)
They wait awhile their wearied limbs to rest,

Till silence should invite them to their feast.
About the hour that Cynthia's *Silver light,*
Had touch'd the pale Meridies of the night;
At last the various Supper being done,
It happened that the Company was gone,
Into a room remote, Servants and all,
To please their nobles fancies with a Ball.
Our host leads forth his stranger, and do's find,
All fitted to the bounties of his mind.
Still on the Table half fill'd dishes stood,
And with delicious bits the floor was strow'd.
The courteous mouse presents him with the best,
And both with fat varieties are blest,
Th' industrious Peasant every where does range,
And thanks the gods for his Life's happy change.
Loe, in the midst of a well fraited Pye,
They both at last glutted and wanton lye.
When see the sad Reverse of prosperous fate,
And what fierce storms on mortal glories wait.
With hideous noise, down the rude servants come,
Six dogs before run barking into th' room;
The wretched gluttons fly with wild affright,
And hate the fulness which retards their flight.
Our trembling Peasant wishes now in vain,
That Rocks and Mountains cover'd him again.
Oh how the change of his poor life he curst!
This, of all lives (said he) is sure the worst.
Give me again, *ye gods*, my Cave and wood;
With peace, let tares and acorns be my food.

A Paraphrase upon the 10th *Epistle of the first
Book of* Horace.

Horace *to* Fuscus Aristius.

HEalth, from the lover of the Country me,
   Health, to the lover of the City thee,
A difference in our souls, this only proves,
In all things else, w' agree like marryed doves.
But the warm nest, and crowded dove-house thou
Dost like; I loosly fly from bough to bough,
And Rivers drink, and all the shining day,
Upon fair Trees, or mossy Rocks I play;
In fine, I live and reign when I retire
From all that you equal with Heaven admire.
Like one at last from the Priests service fled,
Loathing the honie'd Cakes, I long for Bread.
Would I a house for happines erect,
Nature alone should be the Architect.
She'd build it more convenient, then great,
And doubtless in the Country choose her seat.
Is there a place, doth better helps supply,
Against the wounds of Winters cruelty?
Is there an Ayr that gentl'er does asswage
The mad Celestial Dogs, or Lyons rage?
Is it not there that sleep (and only there)
Nor noise without, nor cares within does fear?
Does art through pipes, a purer water bring,
Then that which nature straines into a spring?
Can all your Tap'stries, or your Pictures show
More beauties then in herbs and flowers do grow?

Fountains and trees our wearied Pride do please,
Even in the midst of gilded Palaces.
And in your towns that prospect gives delight,
Which opens round the country to our sight.
Men to the good, from which they rashly fly,
Return at last, and their wild Luxury
Does but in vain with those true joyes contend,
Which Nature did to mankind recommend.
The man who changes gold for burnisht Brass,
Or small right Gems, for larger ones of glass:
Is not, at length, more certain to be made
Ridiculous, and wretched by the trade,
Than he, who sells a solid good, to buy
The painted goods of Pride and Vanity.
If thou be wise, no glorious fortune choose,
Which 'tis but pain to keep, yet grief to loose.
For, when we place even trifles, in the heart,
With trifles too, unwillingly we part.
An humble Roof, plain bed, and homely board,
More clear, untainted pleasures do afford,
Then all the Tumult of vain greatness brings
To Kings, or to the favorites of Kings.
The horned Deer by Nature arm'd so well,
Did with the Horse in common pasture dwell;
And when they fought, the field it alwayes wan,
Till the ambitious Horse begg'd help of Man,
And took the bridle, and thenceforth did reign
Bravely alone, as Lord of all the plain:
But never after could the Rider get
From off his back, or from his mouth the bit.
So they, who poverty too much do fear,

T' avoid that weight, a greater burden bear;
That they might Pow'r above their equals have,
To cruel Masters they themselves enslave.
For Gold, their Liberty exchang'd we see,
That fairest flow'r, which crowns Humanity.
And all this mischief does upon them light,
Only, because they know not how, aright,
That great, but secret, happiness to prize,
That's laid up in a Little, for the Wise:
That is the best, and easiest Estate,
Which to a man sits close, but not too strait;
'Tis like a shooe; it pinches, and it burns,
Too narrow; and too large it overturns.
My dearest friend, stop thy desires at last,
And chearfully enjoy the wealth thou hast.
And, if me still seeking for more you see,
Chide, and reproach, despise and laugh at me.
Money was made, not to command our will,
But all our lawful pleasures to fulfil.
Shame and wo to us, if we' our wealth obey;
The Horse doth with the Horse-man run away.

The Country Life.

Libr. 4. Plantarum.

B Lest be the man (and blest he is) whom e're
(Plac'd far out of the roads of Hope or Fear)
A little Field, and little Garden feeds;
The Field gives all that Frugal Nature needs,
The wealthy Garden liberally bestows
All she can ask, when she luxurious grows.

The specious inconveniences that wait
Upon a life of Business, and of State,
He sees (nor does the sight disturb his rest)
By Fools desired, by wicked men possest.
Thus, thus (and this deserv'd great *Virgils* praise)
The old *Corycian* Yeoman past his daies,
Thus his wise life *Abdolonymus* spent:
Th' Ambassadours which the great Emp'rour sent
To offer him a Crown, with wonder found
The reverend Gard'ner howing of his Ground,
Unwillingly and slow and discontent,
From his lov'd Cottage, to a Throne he went.
And oft he stopt in his tryumphant way,
And oft lookt back, and oft was heard to say
Not without sighs, Alas, I there forsake
A happier Kingdom then I go to take.
Thus *Aglaüs* (a man unknown to men,
But the gods knew and therefore lov'd him Then)
Thus liv'd obscurely then without a Name,
Aglaüs now consign'd t' eternal Fame.
For *Gyges*, the rich King, wicked and great,
Presum'd at wise *Apollos Delphick* seat
Presum'd to ask, Oh thou, the whole Worlds Eye,
See'st thou a Man, that Happier is then I?
The God, who scorn'd to flatter Man, reply'd,
Aglaüs Happier is. But *Gyges* cry'd,
In a proud rage, Who can that *Aglaüs* be?
We have heard as yet of no such King as Hee.
And true it was through the whole Earth around
No King of such a Name was to be found.
Is some old *Hero* of that name alive,

Who his high race does from the Gods derive?
Is it some mighty General that has done,
Wonders in fight, and God-like honours wone?
Is it some man of endless wealth, said he?
None, none of these; who can this *Aglaüs* bee?
After long search and vain inquiries past,
In an obscure *Arcadian* Vale at last,
(The *Arcadian* life has always shady been)
Near *Sopho's* Town (which he but once had seen)
This *Aglaüs* who Monarchs Envy drew,
Whose Happiness the Gods stood witness too,
This mighty *Aglaüs* was labouring found,
With his own Hands in his own little ground.

   So, gracious God, (if it may lawful be,
Among those foolish gods to mention Thee)
So let me act, on such a private stage,
The last dull Scenes of my declining Age;
After long toiles and Voyages in vain,
This quiet Port let my tost Vessel gain,
Of Heavenly rest, this Earnest to me lend,
Let my Life sleep, and learn to love her End.

5. The Garden.

To J. Evelyn *Esquire.*

I Never had any other desire so strong, and so like
to Covetousness as that one which I have had
always, that I might be master at last of a small house
and large garden, with very moderate conveniencies
joyned to them, and there dedicate the remainder of

my life only to the culture of them and study of
Nature,

> And there (with no design beyond my wall) whole
>   and intire to lye,
> In no unactive Ease, and no unglorious Poverty.

Or as *Virgil* has said, Shorter and Better for me,
that I might there *Studiis florere ignobilis otii* (though
I could wish that he had rather said, *Nobilis otii*, when
he spoke of his own) But several accidents of my ill
fortune have disappointed me hitherto, and do still,
of that felicity; for though I have made the first and
hardest step to it, by abandoning all ambitions and
hopes in this World, and by retiring from the noise
of all business and almost company, yet I stick still
in the Inn of a hired House and Garden, among Weeds
and Rubbish; and without that plesantest work of
Human Industry, the Improvement of something which
we call (not very properly, but yet we call) Our Own.
I am gone out from *Sodom*, but I am not yet arrived
at my Little *Zoar*. *O let me escape thither* (*Is it not a
Little one?*) *and my Soul shall live.* I do not look back
yet; but I have been forced to stop, and make too
many halts. You may wonder, Sir, (for this seems a
little too extravagant and Pindarical for *Prose*) what
I mean by all this Preface; It is to let you know, That
though I have mist, like a Chymist, my great End,
yet I account my affections and endeavours well rewarded by something that I have met with by the By;
which is, that they have procured to me some part
in your kindness and esteem; and thereby the honour

of having my Name so advantagiously recommended
to Posterity, by the *Epistle* you are pleased to prefix
to the most useful Book that has been written in that
kind, and which is to last as long as Moneths and Years.

Among many other *Arts* and *Excellencies* which you
enjoy, I am glad to find this Favourite of mine the
most predominant, That you choose this for your Wife,
though you have hundreds of other Arts for your
Concubines; Though you know them, and beget Sons
upon them all (to which you are rich enough to allow
great Legacies) yet the issue of this seemes to be
designed by you to the main of the Estate; you have
taken most pleasure in it, and bestow'd most charges
upon its Education: and I doubt not to see that Book,
which you are pleased to Promise to the World, and
of which you have given us a Large Earnest in your
Calendar, as Accomplisht, as any thing can be expected
from an *Extraordinary Wit*, and no ordinary Expences,
and a long Experience. I know no body that possesses
more private happiness then you do in your Garden;
and yet no man who makes his happiness more publick,
by a free communication of the Art and Knowledge
of it to others. All that I my self am able yet to do,
is onely to recommend to Mankind the search of that
Felicity, which you Instruct them how to Find and to
Enjoy.

I.

Happy art Thou, whom God does bless
With the full choice of thine own Happiness;
And happier yet, because thou'rt blest
With prudence, how to choose the best:

In Books and Gardens thou hast plac'd aright
    (Things which thou well dost understand;
And both dost make with thy laborious hand)
    Thy noble, innocent delight:
And in thy virtuous Wife, where thou again dost meet
    Both pleasures more refin'd and sweet:
    The fairest Garden in her Looks,
    And in her Mind the wisest Books.
Oh, Who would change these soft, yet solid joys,
    For empty shows and senceless noys;
    And all which rank Ambition breeds,
Which seem such beauteous Flowers, and are such
    poisonous Weeds?

2.

When God did Man to his own Likeness make,
As much as Clay, though of the purest kind,
    By the great Potters art refin'd;
    Could the Divine Impression take,
    He thought it fit to place him, where
    A kind of Heaven too did appear,
As far as Earth could such a Likeness bear:
    That man no happiness might want,
Which Earth to her first Master could afford;
    He did a Garden for him plant
By the quick Hand of his Omnipotent Word.
As the chief Help and Joy of human life,
He gave him the first Gift; first, ev'n before a Wife.

3.

For God, the universal Architect,
    'Thad been as easie to erect
A Louvre or Escurial, or a Tower
That might with Heav'n communication hold,
As *Babel* vainly thought to do of old:
    He wanted not the skill or power,
    In the Worlds Fabrick those were shown,
And the Materials were all his own.
But well he knew what place would best agree
With Innocence, and with Felicity:
And we elsewhere still seek for them in vain,
If any part of either yet remain;
If any part of either we expect,
This may our Judgment in the search direct;
God the first Garden made, and the first City, *Cain*.

4.

Oh blessed shades! O gentle cool retreat
    From all th' immoderate Heat,
In which the frantick World does Burn and Sweat!
This does the Lion-Star, Ambitions rage;
This Avarice, the Dogstars Thirst asswage;
Every where else their fatal power we see,
They make and rule Mans wretched Destiny:
    They neither Set, nor Disappear,
    But tyrannize o're all the Year;
Whilst we ne're feel their Flame or Influence here.
    The Birds that dance from Bough to Bough,
    And Sing above in every Tree,
    Are not from Fears and Cares more free,

Then we who Lie, or Sit, or Walk below,
    And should by right be Singers too.
What Princes Quire of Musick can excell
      That which within this shade does dwell?
      To which we nothing Pay or Give,
      They like all other Poets live,
Without reward, or thanks for their obliging pains;
      'Tis well if they become not Prey:
The whistling Winds add their less artfull strains,
And a grave Base the murmuring Fountains play;
Nature does all this Harmony bestow,
      But to our Plants, Arts Musick too,
The Pipe, Theorbo, and Guitarr we owe;
The Lute it self, which once was Green and Mute,
      When *Orpheus* strook th' inspired Lute,
      The Trees danc'd round, and understood
      By Sympathy the Voice of Wood.

5.

These are the Spels that to kind Sleep invite,
And nothing does within resistance make,
      Which yet we moderately take;
      Who would not choose to be awake,
While he's encompast round with such delight,
To th' Ear, the Nose, the Touch, the Tast & Sight?
When *Venus* would her dear *Ascanius* keep
A Prisoner in the Downy Bands of Sleep,
She Od'rous Herbs and Flowers beneath him spread
      As the most soft and sweetest Bed;
Not her own Lap would more have charm'd his Head.
Who, that has Reason, and his Smell,

Would not among Roses and Jasmin dwell,
    Rather then all his Spirits choak
With Exhalations of Durt and Smoak?
    And all th' uncleanness which does drown
In Pestilential Clouds a populous Town?
The Earth it self breaths better Perfumes here,
Then all the Femal Men or Women there,
Not without cause, about them bear.

6.

When *Epicurus* to the World had taught,
    That Pleasure was the chiefest Good,
(And was perhaps i'th' right, if rightly understood)
    His Life he to his Doctrine brought,
And in a Gardens shade that Sovereign Pleasure sought:
Whoever a true Epicure would be,
May there find cheap and virtuous Luxurie.
Vitellius his Table, which did hold
As many Creatures as the Ark of old:
That Fiscal Table, to which every day
All Countries did a constant Tribute pay,
Could nothing more delicious afford,
    Then Natures Liberalitie,
Helpt with a little Art and Industry,
Allows the meanest Gard'ners board.
The wanton Tast no Fish, or Fowl can choose,
For which the Grape or Melon she would lose,
Though all th' Inhabitants of Sea and Air
Be listed in the Gluttons bill of Fare;
    Yet still the Fruits of Earth we see
Plac'd the Third Story high in all her Luxury.

7.

But with no Sence the Garden does comply;
None courts, or flatters, as it does the Eye:
When the great *Hebrew* King did almost strain
The wond'rous Treasures of his Wealth and Brain,
His Royal Southern Guest to entertain;
 Though she on Silver Floores did tread,
With bright *Assyrian* Carpets on them spread,
  To hide the Metals Poverty.
 Though she look'd up to Roofs of Gold,
 And nought around her could behold
  But Silk and rich Embrodery,
  And *Babylonian* Tapestry,
 And wealthy *Hirams* Princely Dy:
Though *Ophirs* Starry Stones met every where her Eye;
Though She her self, and her gay Host were drest
With all the shining glories of the East;
When lavish Art her costly work had done,
 The honour and the Prize of Bravery
Was by the Garden from the Palace won;
And every Rose and Lilly there did stand
 Better attir'd by Natures hand:
The case thus judg'd against the King we see,
By one that would not be so Rich, though Wiser far
 then He.

8.

Nor does this happy place onely dispence
 Such various Pleasures to the Sence;
  Here Health it self does live,
That Salt of Life, which does to all a relish give,

Its standing Pleasure, and Intrinsick Wealth,
The Bodies Virtue, and the Souls good Fortune Health.
The Tree of Life, when it in *Eden* stood,
Did its immortal Head to Heaven rear;
It lasted a tall Cedar till the Flood;
Now a small thorny Shrub it does appear;
  Nor will it thrive too every where:
  It alwayes here is freshest seen;
  'Tis onely here an Ever-green.
  If through the strong and beauteous Fence
  Of Temperance and Innocence,
And wholsome Labours, and a quiet Mind,
  Any Diseases passage find,
  They must not think here to assail
A Land unarm'd, or without a Guard;
They must fight for it, and dispute it hard,
  Before they can prevail:
  Scarce any Plant is growing here
Which against Death some Weapon does not bear.
  Let Cities boast, That they provide
  For Life the Ornaments of Pride;
  But 'tis the Country and the Field,
  That furnish it with Staffe and Shield.

9.

Where does the Wisdom and the Power Divine
In a more bright and sweet Reflection shine?
Where do we finer strokes and colours see
Of the Creators Real Poetry,
  Then when we with attention look
Upon the Third Dayes Volume of the Book?

If we could open and intend our Eye,
    We all like *Moses* should espy
Ev'n in a Bush the radiant Deitie.
But we despise these his Inferiour wayes,
(Though no less full of Miracle and Praise)
    Upon the Flowers of Heaven we gaze;
The Stars of Earth no wonder in us raise,
      Though these perhaps do more then they,
        The life of Mankind sway.
Although no part of mighty Nature be
More stor'd with Beauty, Power, and Mysterie;
Yet to encourage human Industrie,
God has so ordered, that no other part
Such Space, and such Dominion leaves for Art.

10.

We no where Art do so triumphant see,
    As when it Grafs or Buds the Tree:
In other things we count it to excell,
If it a Docile Schollar can appear
To Nature, and but imitate her well;
It over-rules, and is her Master here.
It imitates her Makers Power Divine,
And changes her sometimes, and sometimes does refine:
It does, like Grace, the Fallen Tree restore
To its blest state of Paradise before:
Who would not joy to see his conquering hand
Ore all the Vegetable World command?
And the wild Giants of the Wood receive
    What Law he's pleas'd to give?

He bids th' il-natur'd Crab produce
The gentler Apples Winy Juice;
    The golden fruit that worthy is
    Of *Galatea*'s purple kiss;
    He does the savage Hawthorn teach
    To bear the Medlar and the Pear,
    He bids the rustick Plum to rear
    A noble Trunk, and be a Peach.
    Even *Daphnes* coyness he does mock,
    And weds the Cherry to her stock,
    Though she refus'd *Apolloes* suit;
    Even she, that chast and Virgin Tree,
    Now wonders at her self, to see
That she's a mother made, and blushes in her fruit.

II.

Methinks I see great *Dioclesian* walk
In the *Salonian* Gardens noble shade,
Which by his own Imperial hands was made:
I see him smile (methinks) as he does talk
With the Ambassadors, who come in vain,
    T' entice him to a throne again.
If I, my Friends (said he) should to you show
All the delights, which in these Gardens grow;
'Tis likelier much, that you should with me stay,
Than 'tis that you should carry me away:
And trust me not, my Friends, if every day,
    I walk not here with more delight,
Then ever after the most happy fight,
In Triumph, to the Capitol, I rod,
To thank the gods, & to be thought, my self almost a god.

6. *Of Greatness.*

SInce we cannot attain to Greatness, (saies the *Sieur de Montagn*) let's have our revenge by railing at it: this he spoke but in Jest. I believe he desired it no more then I do, and had less reason, for he enjoyed so plentiful and honourable a fortune in a most excellent Country, as allowed him all the real conveniences of it, seperated and purged from the Incommodities. If I were but in his condition, I should think it hard measure, without being convinced of any crime, to be sequestred from it and made one of the Principal Officers of State. But the Reader may think that what I now say, is of small authority, because I never was, nor ever shall be put to the tryal: I can therefore only make my Protestation,

> *If ever I more Riches did desire*
> *Then Cleanliness and Quiet do require.*
> *If e're Ambition did my Fancy cheat,*
> *With any wish, so mean as to be great,*
> *Continue, Heav'n, still from me to remove*
> *The Humble Blessings of that Life I love.*

I know very many men will despise, and some pity me, for this humour, as a poor spirited fellow; but I'me content, and like *Horace* thank God for being so. *Dii bene fecerunt inopis me quodque pusilli Finxerunt animi.* I confess, I love Littleness almost in all things. A little convenient Estate, a little chearful House, a little Company, and a very little Feast, and if I were ever to fall in love again (which is a great Passion, and

therefore, I hope, I have done with it) it would be,
I think, with Prettiness, rather than with Majestical
Beauty. I would neither wish that my Mistress, nor
my Fortune, should be a *Bona Roba*, nor as *Homer*
uses to describe his Beauties, like a Daughter of great
Jupiter for the stateliness and largeness of her person,
but as *Lucretius* saies,

> *Parvula, pumilio,* Χαρίτων μία, *tota merum sal.*

Where there is one man of this, I believe there are
a thousand of *Senecio's* mind, whose ridiculous affectation of Grandeur, *Seneca* the Elder describes to this
effect. *Senecio* was a man of a turbid and confused
wit, who could not endure to speak any but mighty
words and sentences, till this humour grew at last into
so notorious a Habit, or rather Disease, as became the
sport of the whole Town: he would have no servants,
but huge, massy fellows, no plate or houshold-stuff,
but thrice as big as the fashion: you may believe me,
for I speak it without Railery, his extravagancy came
at last into such a madness, that he would not put
on a pair of shooes, each of which was not big enough
for both his feet: he would eat nothing but what was
great, nor touch any Fruit but Horse-plums and Pound-
pears: he kept a Concubine that was a very Gyantess,
and made her walk too alwaies in *Chiopins*, till at last,
he got the Surname of *Senecio Grandio*, which, *Messala*
said, was not his *Cognomen*, but his *Cognomentum:*
when he declamed for the three hundred *Lacedæmonians*, who alone opposed *Xerxes* his Army of above
three hundred thousand, he stretch'd out his armes,

and stood on tiptoes, that he might appear the taller, and cryed out, in a very loud voice; I rejoyce, I rejoyce— We wondred, I remember, what new great fortune had befaln his Eminence. *Xerxes* (saies he) is All mine own. He who took away the sight of the Sea, with the Canvas Vailes of so many ships— and then he goes on so, as I know not what to make of the rest, whither it be the fault of the Edition, or the Orators own burly way of Non-sence.

This is the character that *Seneca* gives of this *Hyperbolical* Fop, whom we stand amazed at, and yet there are very few men who are not in some things, and to some degrees *Grandio's*. Is any thing more common, then to see our Ladies of quality wear such high shooes as they cannot walk in, without one to lead them? and a Gown as long again as their Body, so that they cannot stir to the next room without a Page or two to hold it up? I may safely say, That all the ostentation of our Grandees is just like a Train of no use in the world, but horribly cumbersome and incommodious. What is all this, but a spice of *Grandio?* how tædious would this be, if we were always bound to it? I do believe there is no King, who would not rather be deposed, than endure every day of his Reign all the Ceremonies of his Coronation. The mightiest Princes are glad to fly often from these Majestique pleasures (which is, methinks, no small disparagement to them) as it were for refuge, to the most contemptible divertisements, and meanest recreations of the vulgar, nay, even of Children. One of the most powerful and fortunate Princes of the world, of late, could finde out no delight so satisfactory, as the keeping of little singing Birds, and hearing of them, and whistling to them. What did the Emperours of the whole world? If ever any men had the free and full enjoyment of all humane Greatness (nay that would not suffice, for they would be gods too) they certainly possest it: and yet, one of them who stiled himself Lord and God of the Earth, could not tell how to pass his whole day pleasantly, without spending constant two or three hours in catching of Flies, and killing them with a bodkin, as if his Godship had been *Beelzebub*. One of his Predecessors, *Nero* (who never put any bounds, nor met with any stop to his Appetite) could divert himself with no pastime more agreeable, than to run about the streets all night in a disguise, and abuse the women, and affront the men whom he met, and sometimes to beat them, and sometimes to be beaten by them: This was one of his Imperial nocturnal pleasures. His chiefest in the day, was to sing and play upon a Fiddle, in the habit of a Minstril, upon the publick stage: he was prouder of the Garlands that were given to his Divine voice (as they called it then) in those kinde of Prizes, than all his Forefathers were, of their Triumphs over nations: He did not at his death complain, that so mighty an Emperour and the last of all the *Cæsarian* race of Deities, should be brought to so shameful and miserable an end, but only cryed out, Alas, what pity 'tis that so excellent a Musician should perish in this manner! His Uncle *Claudius* spent half his time at playing at Dice, that was the main fruit of his Soveraignty. I omit the madnesses of *Caligula*'s

delights, and the execrable sordidness of those of
Tiberius. Would one think that *Augustus* himself, the
highest and most fortunate of mankind, a person
endowed too with many excellent parts of Nature,
should be so hard put to it sometimes for want of
recreations, as to be found playing at Nuts and
bounding stones, with little *Syrian* and *Moorish* Boyes,
whose company he took delight in, for their prating
and their wantonness?

> Was it for this, that *Romes* best blood he spilt,
>   With so much Falshood, so much guilt?
> Was it for this that his Ambition strove,
> To æqual *Cæsar* first, and after *Jove?*
> Greatness is barren sure of solid joyes;
> Her Merchandize (I fear) is all in toyes,
> She could not else sure so uncivil be,
> To treat his universal Majesty,
>   His new-created Deity,
>   With Nuts and Bounding-stones and Boys.

But we must excuse her for this meager entertainment, she has not really wherewithall to make such
Feasts as we imagine, her Guests must be contented
sometimes with but slender Cates, and with the same
cold meats served over and over again, even till they
become Nauseous. When you have pared away all the
Vanity what solid and natural contentment does there
remain which may not be had with five hundred pounds
a year? not so many servants or horses; but a few
good ones, which will do all the business as well: not
so many choice dishes at every meal, but at several

meals, all of them, which makes them both the more
healthy, and the more pleasant: not so rich garments,
nor so frequent changes, but as warm and as comely,
and so frequent change too, as is every jot as good
for the Master, though not for the Tailor, or *Valet de
chambre*: not such a stately Palace, nor guilt rooms,
or the costliest sorts of Tapestry; but a convenient
brick house, with decent Wainscot, and pretty Forest-
work hangings. Lastly, (for I omit all other particulars,
and will end with that which I love most in both
conditions) not whole Woods cut in walks, nor vast
Parks, nor Fountain, or Cascade-Gardens; but herb,
and flower, and fruit-Gardens which are more useful,
and the water every whit as clear and wholesome, as
if it darted from the breasts of a marble Nymph, or
the Urn of a River-God. If for all this, you like better
the substance of that former estate of Life, do but
consider the inseparable accidents of both: Servitude,
Disquiet, Danger, and most commonly Guilt, Inherent
in the one; in the other Liberty, Tranquility, Security
and Innocence, and when you have thought upon this,
you will confess that to be a truth which appeared to
you before, but a ridiculous *Paradox*, that a low
Fortune is better guarded and attended than an high
one, If indeed we look only upon the flourishing Head
of the Tree, it appears a most beautiful object,

>   ——*Sed quantum vertice ad auras
>   Ætherias tantum radice ad Tartara tendit.*

As far as up to'wards He'ven the Branches grow,
So far the Root sinks down to Hell below.

Another horrible disgrace to greatness is, that it is for the most part in pitiful want and distress: what a wonderful thing is this? unless it degenerate into Avarice, and so cease to be Greatness: It falls perpetually into such Necessities, as drive it into all the meanest and most sordid ways of Borrowing, Cousinage, and Robbery, *Mancipiis locuples eget æris Cappadocum Rex*, This is the case of almost all Great men, as well as of the poor King of *Cappadocia*. They abound with slaves, but are indigent of Money. The ancient Roman Emperours, who had the Riches of the whole world for their Revenue, had wherewithal to live (one would have thought) pretty well at ease, and to have been exempt from the pressures of extream Poverty. But yet with most of them, it was much otherwise, and they fell perpetually into such miserable penury, that they were forced to devour or squeeze most of their friends and servants, to cheat with infamous projects, to ransack and pillage all their Provinces. This fashion of Imperial Grandeur, is imitated by all inferiour and subordinate sorts of it, as if it were a point of Honour. They must be cheated of a third part of their Estates, two other thirds they must expend in Vanity, so that they remain Debtors for all the Necessary Provisions of life, and have no way to satisfie those debts, but out of the succours and supplies of Rapine, as Riches encreases (says Solomon) so do the Mouths that devour it. The Master Mouth has no more than before. The Owner, methinks, is like *Ocnus* in the Fable, who is perpetually winding a Rope of Hay and an Ass at the end perpetually eating it. Out of these incon-

veniences arises naturally one more, which is, that no
Greatness can be satisfied or contented with it self: still
if it could mount up a little higher, it would be Happy,
if it could gain but that point, it would obtain all it's
desires; but yet at last, when it is got up to the very
top of the Pic of Tenarif, it is in very great danger
of breaking its neck downwards, but in no possibility
of ascending upwards into the seat of Tranquility above
the Moon. The first ambitious men in the world, the
old Gyants are said to have made an Heroical attempt
of scaling Heaven in despight of the gods, and they
cast *Ossa* upon *Olympus* and *Pelion* upon *Ossa:* two
or three mountains more they thought would have
done their Business, but the Thunder spoild all the
work, when they were come up to the third story.

And what a noble plot was crost,
And what a brave design was lost.

A famous person of their Off-spring, the late Gyant
of our Nation, when from the condition of a very in-
considerable Captain, he had made himself Lieutenant
General of an Army of little *Titans*, which was his
first Mountain, and afterwards General, which was his
second, and after that, absolute Tyrant of three King-
doms, which was the third, and almost touch'd the
Heaven which he affected, is believed to have dyed
with grief and discontent, because he could not attain
to the honest name of a King, and the old formality
of a Crown, though he had before exceeded the power
by a wicked Usurpation. If he could have compast
that, he would perhaps have wanted something else

that is necessary to felicity, and pined away for want
of the Title of an Emperour or a God. The reason of
this is, that Greatness has no reallity in Nature, but
a Creature of the Fancy, a Notion that consists onely
in Relation and Comparison: It is indeed an Idol; but
St. *Paul* teaches us, *That an Idol is nothing in the
World*. There is in truth no Rising or Meridian of the
Sun, but onely in respect to several places: there is
no Right or Left, no Upper-Hand in Nature; every
thing is Little, and every thing is Great, according as
it is diversly compared. There may be perhaps some
Village in *Scotland* or *Ireland* where I might be a Great
Man; and in that case I should be like *Cæsar* (you
would wonder how *Cæsar* and I, should be like one
another in any thing) and choose rather to be the First
man of the Village, then Second at *Rome*. Our Country
is called *Great Britany*, in regard onely of a Lesser
of the same Name; it would be but a ridiculous
Epithete for it, when we consider it together with the
Kingdom of *China*. That too, is but a pitifull Rood
of ground in comparison of the whole Earth besides:
and this whole Globe of Earth, which we account so
immense a Body, is but one Point or Atome in relation
to those numberless Worlds that are scattered up and
down in the Infinite Space of the Skie which we behold.
The other many Inconveniences of grandeur I have
spoken of disperstly in several Chapters, and shall end
this with an *Ode* of *Horace*, not exactly copyed, but
rudely imitated.

Horace. L. 3. Ode 1.

Odi profanum vulgus, &c.

1.

H Ence, ye Profane; I hate ye all;
  Both the Great, Vulgar, and the small.
To Virgin Minds, which yet their Native whiteness hold,
Not yet Discolour'd with the Love of Gold,
    (That Jaundice of the Soul,
Which makes it look so Guilded and so Foul)
To you, ye very Few, these truths I tell;
The Muse inspires my Song, Heark, and observe it well.

2.

We look on Men, and wonder at such odds
    'Twixt things that were the same by Birth;
We look on Kings as Giants of the Earth,
These Giants are but Pigmeys to the Gods.
    The humblest Bush and proudest Oak,
Are but of equal proof against the Thunder-stroke.
Beauty, and Strength, and Wit, and Wealth, and Power
    Have their short flourishing hour;
    And love to see themselves, and smile,
And joy in their Preeminence a while;
    Even so in the same Land,
Poor Weeds, rich Corn, gay Flowers together stand;
Alas, Death Mowes down all with an impartial Hand.

3.

And all you Men, whom Greatness does so please,
    Ye feast (I fear) like *Damocles:*
    If you your eyes could upwards move,

(But you (I fear) think nothing is above)
You would perceive by what a little thread
    The Sword still hangs over your head.
No Tide of Wine would drown your cares;
No Mirth or Musick over-noise your feares.
The fear of Death would you so watchfull keep,
As not t' admit the Image of it, sleep.

4.

Sleep is a God too proud to wait in Palaces
And yet so humble too as not to scorn
    The meanest Country Cottages;
    His Poppey grows among the Corn.
The Halcyon sleep will never build his nest
    In any stormy breast.
    'Tis not enough that he does find
    Clouds and Darkness in their Mind;
    Darkness but half his work will do.
'Tis not enough; he must find Quiet too.

5.

The man, who in all wishes he does make,
    Does onely Natures Counsel take.
That wise and happy man will never fear
    The evil Aspects of the Year;
Nor tremble, though two Comets should appear;
He does not look in Almanacks to see,
    Whether he Fortunate shall be;
Let *Mars* and *Saturn* in th' Heavens conjoyn,
And what they please against the World design,
    So *Jupiter* within him shine.

6.

If of your pleasures and desires no end be found,
God to your Cares and Fears will set no bound.
    What would content you? Who can tell?
Ye fear so much to lose what you have got,
    As if you lik'd it well.
Ye strive for more, as if ye lik'd it not.
    Go, level Hills, and fill up Seas,
Spare nought that may your wanton Fancy please
    But trust Me, when you 'have done all this,
Much will be Missing still, and much will be Amiss.

7. *Of Avarice.*

THere are two sorts of *Avarice*, the one is but of a
Bastard kind, and that is, the rapacious Appetite
of Gain; not for its own sake, but for the pleasure of
refunding it immediately through all the Channels of
Pride and Luxury. The other is the true kind, and
properly so called; which is a restless and unsatiable
desire of Riches, not for any farther end or use, but
onely to hoard, and preserve, and perpetually encrease
them. The Covetous Man, of the first kind, is like a
greedy *Ostrich*, which devours any Metall, but 'tis with
an intent to feed upon it, and in effect it makes a shift
to digest and excern it. The second is like the foolish
Chough, which loves to steal Money onely to hide it.
The first does much harm to Mankind, and a little
good too to some few: The second does good to none;
no, not to himself. The first can make no excuse to
God, or Angels, or Rational Men for his actions:
The second can give no Reason or colour, not to

the Devil himself for what he does; He is a slave to Mammon without wages. The first makes a shift to be beloved; I, and envyed too by some People: The second is the universal Object of Hatred and Contempt. There is no Vice has been so pelted with good Sentences, and especially by the Poets, who have pursued it with Stories and Fables, and Allegories, and Allusions; and moved, as we say, every Stone to fling at it: Among all which, I do not remember a more fine and Gentleman-like Correction, then that which was given it by one Line of *Ovids*.

Desunt Luxuriæ multa, Avaritiæ Omnia.

Much is wanting to Luxury, All to Avarice.

To which saying, I have a mind to add one Member, and render it thus,

Poverty wants some, Luxury Many, Avarice
    All Things.

Some body sayes of a virtuous and wise Man, That having nothing, he has all: This is just his Antipode, Who, having All things, yet has Nothing. He's a Guardian Eunuch to his beloved Gold; *Audivi eos Amatores esse maximos sed nil potesse*. They'r the fondest Lovers, but impotent to Enjoy.

And, oh, What Mans condition can be worse
Then his, whom Plenty starves, and Blessings curse;
The Beggars but a common Fate deplore,
The Rich poor Man's Emphatically Poor.

I wonder how it comes to pass, that there has never been any Law made against him: Against him, do I

say? I mean, For him; as there are publick Provisions
made for all other Madmen: It is very reasonable that
the King should appoint some persons (and I think
the Courtiers would not be against this proposition)
to manage his Estate during his Life (for his Heires
commonly need not that care) and out of it to make
it their business to see, that he should not want Alimony
befitting his condition, which he could never get out
of his own cruel fingers. We relieve idle Vagrants, and
counterfeit Beggars, but have no care at all of these
really Poor men, who are (methinks) to be respectfully
treated in regard of their quality. I might be endless
against them, but I am almost choakt with the superabundance of the Matter; Too much Plenty im-
poverishes me as it does Them. I will conclude this
odious Subject with part of *Horace's* first *Satyre*, which
take in his own familiar stile.

  I 'dmire, *Mæcenas*, how it comes to pass,
  That no man ever yet contented was,
  Nor is, nor perhaps will be with that state
  In which his own choice plants him or his Fate
  Happy the Merchant, the old Soldier cries;
  The Merchant beaten with tempestuous skies,
  Happy the Soldier one half hour to thee
  Gives speedy Death or Glorious victory.
  The Lawyer, knockt up early from his rest
  By restless Clyents, calls the Peasant blest,
  The Peasant when his Labours ill succeed,
  Envys the Mouth which only Talk does feed,
  'Tis not (I think you'l say) that I want store
  Of Instances, if here I add no more,

They are enough to reach at least a mile
Beyond long *Orator Fabias* his Stile.
But, hold, you whom no Fortune e're endears
Gentlemen, Malecontents, and Mutineers,
Who bounteous *Jove* so often cruel call,
Behold, *Jove's* now resolv'd to please you all.
Thou Souldier be a Merchant, Merchant, Thou
A Souldier be; and, Lawyer, to the Plow.
Change all your stations strait, why do you stay?
The Devil a man will change, now when he may,
Were I in General *Jove's* abused case,
By *Jove* I'de cudgel this rebellious race:
But he's too good; Be all then as you were,
However make the best of what you are,
And in that state be chearful and rejoyce,
Which either was your Fate, or was your Choice.
No, they must labour yet, and sweat and toil,
And very miserable be a while.
But 'tis with a Design only to gain
What may their Age with plenteous ease maintain.
The prudent Pismire does this Lesson teach
And industry to Lazy Mankind preach.
The little Drudge does trot about and sweat,
Nor does he strait devour all he can get,
But in his temperate Mouth carries it home
A stock for Winter which he knows must come.
And when the rowling World to Creatures here
Turns up the deform'd wrong side of the Year,
And shuts him in, with storms, and cold, and wet,
He chearfully does his past labours eat:
O, does he so? your wise example, th' Ant,

Does not at all times Rest, and Plenty want.
But weighing justly 'a mortal Ants condition
Divides his Life 'twixt Labour and Fruition.
Thee neither heat, nor storms, nor wet, nor cold
From thy unnatural diligence can withhold,
To th' *Indies* thou wouldst run rather then see
Another, though a Friend, Richer then Thee.
Fond man! what Good or Beauty can be found
In heaps of Treasure buried under ground?
Which rather then diminisht e're to see
Thou wouldst thy self too buried with them be:
And what's the difference, is't not quite as bad
Never to Use, as never to have Had?
In thy vast Barns millions of Quarters store,
Thy Belly for all that will hold no more
Then Mine does; every Baker makes much Bread,
What then? He's with no more then others fed.
Do you within the bounds of Nature Live,
And to augment your own you need not strive,
One hundred Acres will no less for you
Your Life's whole business then ten thousand do.
But pleasant 'tis to take from a great store;
What, Man? though you'r resolv'd to take no more
Then I do from a small one? if your Will
Be but a Pitcher or a Pot to fill,
To some great River for it must you go,
When a clear spring just at your feet does flow?
Give me the Spring which does to humane use
Safe, easie, and untroubled stores produce,
He who scorns these, and needs will drink at *Nile*
Must run the danger of the Crocodile,

And of the rapid stream it self which may
At unawares bear him perhaps away.
In a full Flood *Tantalus* stands, his skin
Washt o're in vain, for ever, dry within;
He catches at the Stream with greedy lips,
From his toucht Mouth the wanton Torment slips:
You laugh now, and expand your careful brow;
Tis finely said, but what's all this to you?
Change but the Name, this Fable is thy story,
Thou in a Flood of useless Wealth dost Glory,
Which thou canst only touch but never taste;
Th' abundance still, and still the want does last.
The Treasures of the Gods thou wouldst not spare,
But when they'r made thine own, they Sacred are,
And must be kept with reverence, as if thou
No other use of precious Gold didst know,
But that of curious Pictures to delight
With the fair stamp thy *Virtuoso* sight.
The only true, and genuine use is this,
To buy the things which *Nature* cannot miss
Without discomfort, Oyl, and vital Bread,
And Wine by which the Life of Life is fed.
And all those few things else by which we live;
All that remains is Giv'n for thee to Give;
If Cares and Troubles, Envy, Grief and Fear,
The bitter Fruits be, which fair Riches bear,
If a new Poverty grow out of store;
The old plain way, ye Gods, let me be Poor.

A Paraphrase on an Ode in Horace's *third Book,*
beginning thus, Inclusam Danaen turris ahenea.

A Tower of Brass, one would have said,
  And Locks, and Bolts, and Iron bars,
And Guards, as strict as in the heat of wars,
Might have preserv'd one Innocent Maiden-head.
The jealous Father thought he well might spare,
      All further jealous Care,
And as he walkt, t' himself alone he smil'd,
      To think how *Venus* Arts he had beguil'd;
      And when he slept, his rest was deep,
But *Venus* laugh'd to see and hear him sleep.
      She taught the Amorous *Jove*
      A Magical receit in Love,
Which arm'd him stronger, and which help'd him more,
Than all his Thunder did, and his Almighty-ship before.

2.

She taught him Loves Elixar, by which Art,
His Godhead into Gold he did convert,
      No Guards did then his passage stay,
      He pass'd with ease; Gold was the Word;
Subtle as Lightning, bright and quick and fierce,
      Gold through Doors and Walls did pierce;
And as that works sometimes upon the sword,
      Melted the Maiden-head away,
Even in the secret scabbard where it lay.
      The prudent *Macedonian* King,
To blow up Towns, a Golden Mine did spring.
      He broke through Gates with this *Petar*,

'Tis the great Art of Peace, the Engine 'tis of War;
      And Fleets and Armies follow it afar,
The Ensign 'tis at Land, and 'tis the Seamans Star.

3.

Let all the World, slave to this Tyrant be,
Creature to this Disguised Deitie,
      Yet it shall never conquer me.
A Guard of Virtues will not let it pass,
And wisdom is a Tower of stronger brass.
The Muses Lawrel round my Temples spread,
'T does from this Lightnings force secure my head.
      Nor will I lift it up so high,
As in the violent Meteors way to lye.
Wealth for its power do we honour and adore?
The things we hate, ill Fate, and Death, have more.

4.

From Towns and Courts, Camps of the Rich and Great,
The vast *Xerxean* Army I retreat,
And to the small Laconick forces fly,
      Which hold the straights of Poverty.
Sellars and Granaries in vain we fill,
      With all the bounteous Summers store,
If the Mind thirst and hunger still.
      The poor rich Man's emphatically poor.
      Slaves to the things we too much prize,
We Masters grow of all that we despise.

5.

A Field of Corn, a Fountain and a Wood,
      Is all the Wealth by Nature understood,

The Monarch on whom fertile *Nile* bestows
  All which that grateful Earth can bear,
  Deceives himself, if he suppose
That more than this falls to his share.
Whatever an Estate does beyond this afford,
  Is not a rent paid to the Lord;
But is a Tax illegal and unjust,
Exacted from it by the Tyrant Lust.
  Much will always wanting be,
  To him who much desires. Thrice happy He
To whom the wise indulgency of Heaven,
 With sparing hand, but just enough has given.

8. *The dangers of an Honest man in much Company.*

I F twenty thousand naked *Americans* were not able to resist the assaults of but twenty well-armed *Spaniards*, I see little possibility for one Honest man to defend himself against twenty thousand Knaves, who are all furnisht *Cap a pe*, with the defensive arms of worldly prudence, and the offensive too of craft and malice. He will find no less odds than this against him, if he have much to do in humane affairs. The only advice therefore which I can give him, is, to be sure not to venture his person any longer in the open Campagn, to retreat and entrench himself, to stop up all Avenues, and draw up all bridges against so numerous an Enemy. The truth of it is, that a man in much business must either make himself a Knave, or else the world will make him a Fool: and if the injury

went no farther then the being laught at, a wise man
would content himself with the revenge of retaliation;
but the case is much worse, for these civil *Cannibals*
too, as well as the wild ones, not only dance about
such a taken stranger, but at last devour him. A sober
man cannot get too soon out of drunken company,
though they be never so kind and merry among themselves, 'tis not unpleasant only, but dangerous to him.
Do ye wonder that a vertuous man should love to be
alone? It is hard for him to be otherwise; he is so,
when he is among ten thousand: neither is the Solitude
so uncomfortable to be alone without any other
creature, as it is to be alone, in the midst of wild
Beasts. Man is to man all kinde of Beasts, a fauning
Dog, a roaring Lion, a theiving Fox, a robbing Wolf,
a dissembling Crocodile, a treacherous Decoy, and a
rapacious Vulture. The civilest, methinks, of all
Nations, are those whom we account the most barbarous, there is some moderation and good Nature in
the *Toupinambaltians* who eat no men but their
Enemies, whilst we learned and polite and Christian
Europeans, like so many Pikes and Sharks prey upon
every thing that we can swallow. It is the great boast
of Eloquence and Philosophy, that they first con-
gregated men disperst, united them into Societies, and
built up the Houses and the walls of Cities. I wish they
could unravel all they had wooven; that we might have
our Woods and our Innocence again instead of our
Castles and our Policies. They have assembled many
thousands of scattered people into one body: 'tis true,
they have done so, they have brought them together

into Cities, to cozen, and into Armies to murder one
another: They found them Hunters and Fishers of
wild creatures, they have made them Hunters and
Fishers of their Brethren, they boast to have reduced
them to a State of Peace, when the truth is, they have
only taught them an Art of War; they have framed,
I must confess, wholesome laws for the restraint of
Vice, but they rais'd first that Devil which now they
Conjure and cannot Bind; though there were before
no punishments for wickednes, yet there was less com-
mitted because there were no Rewards for it. But the
men who praise Philosophy from this Topick are much
deceived; let Oratory answer for it self, the tinckling
perhaps of that may unite a Swarm: it never was the
work of Philosophy to assemble multitudes, but to
regulate onely, and govern them when they were
assembled, to make the best of an evil, and bring them,
as much as is possible, to Unity again. Avarice and
Ambition only were the first Builders of Towns, and
Founders of Empire; They said, *Go to, let us build us
a City and a Tower whose top may reach unto heaven,
and let us make us a name, least we be scattered abroad
upon the face of the Earth.* What was the beginning of
Rome, the *Metropolis* of all the World? what was it,
but a concourse of Theives, and a Sanctuary of
Criminals? it was justly named by the *Augury* of no
less then twelve Vultures, and the Founder cimented
his walls with the blood of his Brother; not unlike to
this was the beginning even of the first Town too in
the world, and such is the Original sin of most Cities:
their Actual encrease daily with their Age and growth;

the more people, the more wicked all of them; every one brings in his part to enflame the contagion, which becomes at last so universal and so strong, that no Precepts can be sufficient Preservatives, nor any thing secure our safety, but flight from among the Infected. We ought in the choice of a Scituation to regard above all things the Healthfulness of the place, and the healthfulness of it for the Mind rather than for the Body. But suppose (which is hardly to be supposed) we had Antidote enough against this Poison; nay, suppose farther, we were alwaies and at all pieces armed and provided both against the Assaults of Hostility, and the Mines of Treachery, 'twill yet be but an uncomfortable life to be ever in Alarms, though we were compast round with Fire, to defend ourselves from wild Beasts, the Lodging would be unpleasant, because we must always be obliged to watch that fire, and to fear no less the defects of our Guard, then the diligences of our Enemy. The summe of this is, that a virtuous man is in danger to be trod upon and destroyed in the crowd of his Contraries, nay, which is worse, to be changed and corrupted by them, and that 'tis impossible to escape both these inconveniences without so much caution, as will take away the whole Quiet, that is, the Happiness of his Life. Ye see then, what he may lose, but, I pray, What can he get there? *Quid Romæ faciam? Mentiri nescio.* What should a man of truth and honesty do at Rome? he can neither understand, nor speak the Language of the place; a naked man may swim in the Sea, but 'tis not the way to catch Fish there; they are likelier to devour him,

then he them, if he bring no Nets, and use no Deceits.
I think therefore it was wise and friendly advice which
Martial gave to *Fabian*, when he met him newly
arrived at *Rome*.

> Honest and Poor, faithful in word and thought;
> What has thee, *Fabian*, to the City brought?
> Thou neither the Buffoon, nor Bawd canst play,
> Nor with false whispers th' Innocent betray:
> Nor corrupt Wives, nor from rich Beldams get
> A living by thy industry and sweat;
> Nor with vain promises and projects cheat,
> Nor Bribe or Flatter any of the Great.
> But you'r a Man of Learning, prudent, just;
> A Man of Courage, firm, and fit for trust.
> Why you may stay, and live unenvyed here;
> But (faith) go back, and keep you where you were.

Nay, if nothing of all this were in the case, yet the
very sight of Uncleanness is loathsome to the Cleanly;
the sight of Folly and Impiety vexatious to the Wise
and Pious.

Lucretius, by his favour, though a good Poet; was
but an ill-natur'd Man, when he said, It was delightful
to see other Men in a great storm: And no less ill-
natur'd should I think *Democritus*, who laught at all
the World, but that he retired himself so much out
of it, that we may perceive he took no great pleasure
in that kind of Mirth. I have been drawn twice or
thrice by company to go to *Bedlam*, and have seen
others very much delighted with the fantastical ex-
travagancie of so many various madnesses, which

upon me wrought so contrary an effect, that I alwayes
returned, not onely melancholy, but ev'n sick with the
sight. My compassion there was perhaps too tender,
for I meet a thousand Madmen abroad, without any
perturbation; though, to weigh the matter justly, the
total loss of Reason is less deplorable then the total
depravation of it. An exact Judge of human blessings,
of Riches, Honours, Beauty, even of Wit it self, should
pity the abuse of them more then the want.

Briefly, though a wise man could pass never so
securely through the great Roads of human Life, yet
he will meet perpetually with so many objects and
occasions of compassion, grief, shame, anger, hatred,
indignation, and all passions but envy (for he will find
nothing to deserve that) that he had better strike into
some private path; nay, go so far, if he could, out of
the common way, *Ut nec facta audiat Pelopidarum*;
that he might not so much as hear of the actions of
the Sons of *Adam*. But, Whither shall we flye then?
into the Deserts, like the antient Hermites?

> *Qua terra patet fera regnat Erynnis,*
> *In facinus jurasse putes.*

One would think that all Mankind had bound themselves by an Oath to do all the wickedness they can;
that they had all (as the Scripture speaks) sold themselves to Sin: the difference onely is, that some are a
little more crafty (and but a little God knows) in
making of the bargain. I thought when I went first
to dwell in the Country, that without doubt I should
have met there with the simplicity of the old Poetical

Golden Age: I thought to have found no Inhabitants
there, but such as the Shepherds of Sir *Phil. Sydney*
in *Arcadia*, or of *Monsieur d'Urfe* upon the Banks of
Lignon; and began to consider with my self, which
way I might recommend no less to Posterity the
Happiness and Innocence of the Men of *Chertsea:* but
to confess the truth, I perceived quickly, by infallible
demonstrations, that I was still in Old *England*, and
not in *Arcadia*, or *La Forrest*; that if I could not
content my self with any thing less then exact Fidelity
in human conversation, I had almost as good go back
and seek for it in the Court, or the Exchange, or
Westminster-Hall. I ask again then Whither shall we
fly, or what shall we do? The World may so come in a
Mans way, that he cannot choose but Salute it, he
must take heed though not to go a whoring after it.
If by any lawful Vocation, or just necessity men
happen to be Married to it, I can onely give them
St. *Pauls* advice. *Brethren, the time is short, it remaines
that they that have Wives be as though they had none.
But I would that all Men were even as I my self.*

In all cases they must be sure that they do *Mundum
ducere*, and not *Mundo nubere*. They must retain the
Superiority and Headship over it: Happy are they who
can get out of the sight of this Deceitful Beauty, that
they may not be led so much as into Temptation; who
have not onely quitted the Metropolis, but can abstain
from ever seeing the next Market Town of their
Country.

Claudian's Old Man of *Verona*.

HAppy the Man, who his whole time doth bound
Within th' enclosure of his little ground.
Happy the Man, whom the same humble place,
(Th' hereditary Cottage of his Race)
From his first rising infancy has known,
And by degrees sees gently bending down,
With natural propension to that Earth
Which both preserv'd his Life, and gave him birth.
Him no false distant lights by fortune set,
Could ever into foolish wandrings get.
He never dangers either saw, or fear'd:
The dreadful stormes at Sea he never heard.
He never heard the shrill allarms of War,
Or the worse noises of the Lawyers Bar.
No change of Consuls marks to him the year,
The change of seasons is his Calendar.
The Cold and Heat, Winter and Summer shows,
Autumn by Fruits, and Spring by Flow'rs he knows.
He measures Time by Land-marks, and has found
For the whole day the Dial of his ground.
A neighbouring Wood born with himself he sees,
And loves his old contemporary Trees.
H'as only heard of near *Verona*'s Name,
And knows it like the *Indies*, but by Fame.
Does with a like concernment notice take
Of the Red-Sea, and of *Benacus* Lake.
Thus Health and Strength he to' a third age enjoyes,
And sees a long Posterity of Boys.
About the spacious World let others roam,
The Voyage Life is longest made at home.

9. *The shortness of Life and uncertainty of Riches.*

IF you should see a man who were to cross from *Dover* to *Calais*, run about very busie and sollicitous, and trouble himselfe many weeks before in making provisions for his voyage, would you commend him for a cautious and discreet person, or laugh at him for a timerous and impertinent Coxcomb? A man who is excessive in his pains and diligence, and who consumes the greatest part of his time in furnishing the remainder with all conveniencies and even superfluities, is to Angels and wise men no less ridiculous; he does as little consider the shortness of his passage that he might proportion his cares accordingly. It is, alas, so narrow a streight betwixt the Womb and the Grave, that it might be called the *Pas de Vie*, as well as that the *Pas de Calais*. We are all Ἐφήμεροι (as *Pindar* calls us) Creatures of a day, and therefore our Saviour bounds our desires to that little space; as if it were very probable that every day should be our last, we are taught to demand even Bread for no longer a time. The Sun ought not to set upon our Covetousness no more then upon our Anger, but as to God Almighty a thousand years are as one day, so in direct opposition, one day to the covetous man is as a thousand years; *Tam brevi fortis jaculatur ævo multa*, so far he shoots beyond his Butt: One would think he were of the opinion of the *Millenaries*, and hoped for so long a Reign upon Earth. The Patriarchs before the Flood, who enjoy'd almost such a Life, made, we are sure, less stores for the maintaining of it; they who lived

Nine hundred years scarcely provided for a few days;
we who live but a few days, provide at least for Nine
hundred years; what a strange alteration is this of
Humane Life and Manners? and yet we see an imita-
tion of it in every mans particular experience, for we
begin not the cares of Life till it be half spent, and
still encrease them as that decreases. What is there
among the actions of Beasts so illogical and repugnant
to Reason? when they do any thing which seems to
proceed from that which we call Reason, we disdain
to allow them that perfection, and attribute it only to
a Natural Instinct; and are not we Fools too by the
same kind of Instinct? If we could but learn to
number our days (as we are taught to pray that we
might) we should adjust much better our other accounts, but whilst we never consider an end of them,
it is no wonder if our cares for them be without end
too. *Horace* advises very wisely, and in excellent good
words, *spatio brevi spem longam reseces*, From a short
Life cut off all Hopes that grow too long. They must
be pruned away like suckers that choak the Mother-
Plant, and hinder it from bearing fruit. And in another
place to the same sence, *Vitæ summa brevis spem nos
vetat inchoare longam*, which *Seneca* does not mend
when he says, *Oh quanta dementia est spes longas
inchoantium*! but he gives an example there of an
acquaintance of his named *Senecio*, who from a very
mean beginning by great industry in turning about of
Money through all ways of gain, had attained to
extraordinary Riches but died on a suddain after,
having supped merrily, *In ipso actu bené cedentium*

rerum, in ipso procurrentis fortunæ impetu, In the full
course of his good Fortune, when she had a high Tide
and a stiff Gale and all her Sails on; upon which occasion he cries, out of *Virgil*

> *Insere nunc Melibœe pyros, pone ordine vites,*

> Go *Melibœus*, now,
> Go graff thy Orchards and thy Vineyards plant;
> Behold the Fruit!

For this *Senecio* I have no compassion, because he
was taken as we say, in *ipso facto*, still labouring in
the work of Avarice, but the poor rich man in St. *Luke*
(whose case was not like this) I could pity, methinks,
if the Scripture would permit me, for he seems to have
been satisfied at last, he confesses he had enough for
many years, he bids his soul take its ease, and yet for
all that, God says to him: *Thou Fool, this night thy
soul shall be required of thee,* and the things thou hast
laid up, whom shall they belong to? where shall we
find the causes of this bitter Reproach and terrible
Judgement? we may find, I think, Two, and God
perhaps saw more. First, that he did not intend true
Rest to his Soul, but only to change the employments
of it from Avarice to Luxury, his design is to eat and
to drink, and to be merry. Secondly, that he went on
too long before he thought of resting; the fulness of
his old Barns had not sufficed him, he would stay till
he was forced to build new ones; and God meted out
to him in the same measure; Since he would have
more Riches then his Life could contain, God destroy'd
his Life and gave the Fruits of it to another.

Thus God takes away sometimes the Man from his
Riches, and no less frequently Riches from the Man;
what hope can there be of such a Marriage, where
both parties are so fickle and uncertain? by what Bonds
can such a couple be kept long together?

1.

Why dost thou heap up Wealth, which thou must quit,
    Or, what is worse, be left by it?
Why dost thou load thy self, when thou'rt to flie,
    Oh Man ordain'd to die?

2.

Why dost thou build up stately Rooms on high,
    Thou who art under Ground to lie?
Thou Sow'st and Plantest, but no Fruit must see,
    For Death, alas! is sowing Thee.

3.

Suppose, thou Fortune couldst to tameness bring,
    And clip or pinion her wing;
Suppose thou couldst on Fate so far prevail
    As not to cut off thy Entail.

4.

Yet Death at all that subtilty will laugh,
    Death will that foolish Gardner mock,
Who does a slight and annual Plant engraff,
    Upon a lasting stock.

5.

Thou dost thy self Wise and Industrious deem;
    A mighty Husband thou wouldst seem;
Fond Man! like a bought slave, thou all the while
    Dost but for others Sweat and Toil.

6.

Officious Fool! that needs must medling be
    In business that concerns not thee!
For when to Future years thou' extendst thy cares
    Thou deal'st in other mens affairs.

7.

Even aged men, as if they truly were
    Children again, for Age prepare,
Provisions for long travail they design,
    In the last point of their short Line.

8.

Wisely the Ant against poor Winter hoords
    The stock which Summers wealth affords,
In Grashoppers that must at Autumn die,
    How vain were such an Industry?

9.

Of Power and Honour the deceitful Light
    Might halfe excuse our cheated sight,
If it of Life the whole small time would stay,
    And be our Sun-shine all the day,

10.

Like Lightning that, begot but in a Cloud
    (Though shining bright, and speaking loud)
Whilst it begins, concludes its violent Race,
    And where it Guilds, it wounds the place.

11.

Oh Scene of Fortune, which dost fair appear,
    Only to men that stand not near!
Proud Poverty, that Tinsel brav'ry wears!
    And, like a Rainbow, Painted Tears!

12.

Be prudent, and the shore in prospect keep,
    In a weak Boat trust not the deep.
Plac'd beneath Envy, above envying rise;
    Pity Great Men, Great Things despise.

13.

The wise example of the Heavenly Lark,
    Thy Fellow-Poet, *Cowley* mark,
Above the Clouds let thy proud Musique sound,
    Thy humble Nest build on the Ground.

10. The danger of Procrastination.

A Letter to Mr. S. L.

I Am glad that you approve and applaud my design,
of withdrawing my self from all tumult and business
of the world; and consecrating the little rest of my
time to those studies, to which Nature had so Motherly
inclined me, and from which Fortune, like a Step-
mother has so long detained me. But nevertheless (you

say, which, *But*, is *Ærugo mera*, a rust which spoils
the good Metal it grows upon. But you say) you
would advise me not to precipitate that resolution,
but to stay a while longer with patience and complaisance, till I had gotten such an Estate as might
afford me (according to the saying of that person whom
you and I love very much, and would believe as soon
as another man) *Cum dignitate otium*. This were
excellent advice to *Josua*, who could bid the Sun
stay too. But there's no fooling with Life when it is
once turn'd beyond Forty. The seeking for a Fortune
then, is but a desperate After-game, 'tis a hundred to
one, if a man fling two Sixes and recover all; especially,
if his hand be no luckier than mine. There is some help
for all the defects of Fortune, for if a man cannot
attain to the length of his wishes, he may have his
Remedy by cutting of them shorter. *Epicurus* writes
a Letter to *Idomeneus* (who was then a very powerful,
wealthy, and (it seems) bountiful person) to recommend to Him who had made so many men Rich, one
Pythocles, a friend of his, whom he desired might be
made a rich man too; But I intreat you that you would
not do it just the same way as you have done to many
less deserving persons, but in the most Gentlemanly
manner of obliging him, which is not to adde any
thing to his Estate, but to take something from his
desires. The summ of this is, That for the uncertain
hopes of some Conveniences we ought not to defer the
execution of a work that is Necessary, especially, when
the use of those things which we would stay for, may
otherwise be supplyed, but the loss of time, never

recovered: Nay, farther yet, though we were sure to obtain all that we had a mind to, though we were sure of getting never so much by continuing the Game, yet when the light of Life is so near going out, and ought to be so precious, *Le jeu ne vaut pas la Chandele*, The play is not worth the expence of the Candle: after having been long tost in a Tempest, if our Masts be standing, and we have still Sail and Tackling enough to carry us to our Port, it is no matter for the want of Streamers and Top-Gallants; *Utere velis, Totos pande sinus.* A Gentleman in our late Civil Wars, when his Quarters were beaten up by the Enemy, was taken Prisoner, and lòst his life afterwards, only by staying to put on a Band, and adjust his Periwig: He would escape like a person of quality, or not at all, and dyed the noble Martyr of Ceremony, and Gentility. I think your counsel of *Festina lente* is as ill to a man who is flying from the world, as it would have been to that unfortunate wel-bred Gentleman, who was so cautious as not to fly undecently from his Enemies, and therefore I prefer *Horace's* advice before yours.

— *Sapere Aude, Incipe* —

Begin; the Getting out of doors is the greatest part of the Journey. *Varro* teaches us that *Latin* Proverb, *Portam itineri longissimam esse:* But to return to *Horace*,

> — *Sapere aude,*
> *Incipe, vivendi qui recte prorogat horam*
> *Rusticus expectat dum labitur Amnis, at ille*
> *Labitur, & labetur in omne volubilis ævum.*

Begin, be bold, and venture to be wise;
He who defers this work from day to day,
Does on a Rivers Bank expecting stay,
Till the whole stream, which stopt him, should be gon,
That runs, and as it runs, forever will run on.

Cæsar (the man of Expedition above all others) was
so far from this Folly, that whensoever, in a journey
he was to cross any River, he never went one foot
out of his way for a Bridge, or a Foord, or a Ferry, but
flung himself into it immediately, and swam over;
and this is the course we ought to imitate, if we meet
with any stops in our way to Happiness. Stay till the
waters are low, stay till some Boats come by to
transport you, stay till a Bridge be built for you; You
had even as good stay till the River be quite past.
Persius (who, you use to say, you do not know whether
he be a good Poet or no, because you cannot understand him, and whom therefore (I say) I know to be
not a good Poet) has an odd expression of these
Procrastinators, which, methinks, is full of Fancy.

*Jam Cras Hesternum consumpsimus, Ecce aliud Cras
Egerit hos annos.*

Our Yesterdays To morrow now is gone,
And still a new Tomorrow does come on,
We by Tomorrows draw up all our store,
Till the exhausted Well can yield no more.

And now, I think, I am even with you, for your
Otium cum dignitate, and *Festina lente*, and three or
four other more of your New Latine Sentences: if I
should draw upon you all my forces out of *Seneca* and

Plutarch upon this subject, I should overwhelm you, but I leave those as Triary for your next charge. I shall only give you now a light skirmish out of an Epigrammatist, your special good Friend, and so, *Vale*.

Mart. Lib. 5. Epigr. 59.

To morrow you will Live, you always cry;
In what far Country does this morrow lye,
That 'tis so mighty long 'ere it arrive?
Beyond the *Indies* does this Morrow live?
'Tis so far fetcht this Morrow, that I fear
'Twill be both very Old and very Dear.
To morrow I will live, the Fool does say;
To Day it self's too Late, the wise liv'd Yesterday.

Mart. Lib. 2. Ep. 90.

Wonder not, Sir (you who instruct the Town
In the true Wisdom of the Sacred Gown)
That I make haste to live, and cannot hold
Patiently out, till I grow Rich and Old.
Life for Delays and Doubts no time does give,
None ever yet, made Haste enough to Live.
Let him defer it, whose preposterous care
Omits himself, and reaches to his Heir.
Who does his Fathers bounded stores despise,
And whom his own too never can suffice:
My humble thoughts no glittering roofs require,
Or Rooms that shine with ought but constant Fire.
I well content the Avarice of my sight
With the fair guildings of reflected Light:

Pleasures abroad, the sport of Nature yeilds
Her living Fountains, and her smiling Fields:
And then at home, what pleasure is't to see
A little cleanly chearful Familie?
Which if a chast Wife crown, no less in Her
Then Fortune, I the Golden Mean prefer.
Too noble, nor too wise, she should not be,
No, not too Rich, too Fair, too fond of me.
Thus let my life slide silently away,
With Sleep all Night, and Quiet all the Day.

11. *Of My self.*

IT is a hard and nice Subject for a man to write of
himself, it grates his own heart to say any thing
of disparagement, and the Readers Eares to hear any
thing of praise from him. There is no danger from me
of offending him in this kind; neither my Mind, nor
my Body, nor my Fortune, allow me any materials
for that Vanity. It is sufficient, for my own contentment, that they have preserved me from being
scandalous, or remarkable on the defective side. But
besides that, I shall here speak of myself, only in
relation to the subject of these precedent discourses,
and shall be likelier thereby to fall into the contempt,
then rise up to the estimation of most people. As far
as my Memory can return back into my past Life,
before I knew, or was capable of guessing what the
world, or glories, or business of it were, the natural
affections of my soul gave me a secret bent of aversion
from them, as some Plants are said to turn away from

others, by an Antipathy imperceptible to themselves, and inscrutable to mans understanding. Even when I was a very young Boy at School, instead of running about on Holy-daies and playing with my fellows; I was wont to steal from them, and walk into the fields, either alone with a Book, or with some one Companion, if I could find any of the same temper. I was then too, so much an Enemy to all constraint, that my Masters could never prevail on me, by any perswasions or encouragements, to learn without Book the common rules of Grammar, in which they dispensed with me alone, because they found I made a shift to do the usual exercise out of my own reading and observation. That I was then of the same mind as I am now (which I confess, I wonder at my self) may appear by the latter end of an Ode, which I made when I was but thirteen years old, and which was then printed with many other Verses. The Beginning of it is Boyish, but of this part which I here set down (if a very little were corrected) I should hardly now be much ashamed.

9.

This only grant me, that my means may lye
Too low for Envy, for Contempt too high.
  Some Honor I would have
Not from great deeds, but good alone.
The unknown are better than ill known.
  Rumour can ope' the Grave,
Acquaintance I would have, but when 't depends
Not on the number, but the choice of Friends.

10.

Books should, not business entertain the Light,
And sleep, as undisturb'd as Death, the Night.
    My House a Cottage, more
Then Palace, and should fitting be
For all my Use, no Luxury.
    My Garden painted o're
With Natures hand, not Arts; and pleasures yeild,
Horace might envy in his Sabine field.

11.

Thus would I double my Lifes fading space,
For he that runs it well, twice runs his race.
    And in this true delight,
These unbought sports, this happy State,
I would not fear nor wish my fate,
    But boldly say each night,
To morrow let my Sun his beams display,
Or in clouds hide them; I have liv'd to Day.

You may see by it, I was even then acquainted with
the Poets (for the Conclusion is taken out of *Horace*;)
and perhaps it was the immature and immoderate love
of them which stampt first, or rather engraved these
Characters in me: They were like Letters cut into the
Bark of a young Tree, which with the Tree still grow
proportionably. But, how this love came to be pro-
duced in me so early, is a hard question: I believe I
can tell the particular little chance that filled my head
first with such Chimes of Verse, as have never since
left ringing there: For I remember when I began to
read, and to take some pleasure in it, there was wont

to lie in my Mothers Parlour (I know not by what
accident, for she her self never in her life read any
Book but of Devotion) but there was wont to lie
Spencers Works; this I happened to fall upon, and was
infinitely delighted with the Stories of the Knights,
and Giants, and Monsters, and brave Houses, which
I found every where there: (Though my understanding
had little to do with all this) and by degrees with the
tinckling of the Rhyme and Dance of the Numbers, so
that I think I had read him all over before I was twelve
years old, and was thus made a Poet as irremediably[1]
as a Child is made an Eunuch. With these affections
of mind, and my heart wholly set upon Letters, I
went to the University; But was soon torn from thence
by that violent Publick storm which would suffer
nothing to stand where it did, but rooted up every
Plant, even from the Princely Cedars to Me, the
Hyssop. Yet I had as good fortune as could have
befallen me in such a Tempest; for I was cast by it
into the Family of one of the best Persons, and into
the Court of one of the best Princesses of the World.
Now though I was here engaged in wayes most contrary
to the Original design of my life, that is, into much
company, and no small business, and into a daily sight
of Greatness, both Militant and Triumphant (for that
was the state then of the *English* and *French* Courts)
yet all this was so far from altering my Opinion, that
it onely added the confirmation of Reason to that
which was before but Natural Inclination. I saw plainly
all the Paint of that kind of Life, the nearer I came to

[1] So 1668, altered in the Errata to *immediately*.

it; and that Beauty which I did not fall in Love with, when, for ought I knew, it was reall, was not like to bewitch, or intice me, when I saw that it was Adulterate. I met with several great Persons, whom I liked very well, but could not perceive that any part of their Greatness was to be liked or desired, no more then I would be glad, or content to be in a Storm, though I saw many˙ Ships which rid safely and bravely in it: A storm would not agree with my stomach, if it did with my Courage. Though I was in a croud of as good company as could be found any where, though I was in business of great and honourable trust, though I eate at the best Table, and enjoyed the best conveniences for present subsistance that ought to be desired by a man of my condition in banishment and publick distresses; yet I could not abstain from renewing my old School-boys Wish in a Copy of Verses to the same effect.

> Well then; I now do plainly see
> This busie World and I shall ne're agree, *&c*

And I never then proposed to my self any other advantage from His Majesties Happy Restoration, but the getting into some moderately convenient Retreat in the Country, which I thought in that case I might easily have compassed, as well as some others, with no greater probabilities or pretences have arrived to extraordinary fortunes: But I had before written a shrewd Prophesie against my self, and I think *Apollo* inspired me in the Truth, though not in the Elegance of it.

Thou, neither great at Court nor in the War,
Nor at th' Exchange shal't be, nor at the wrangling Barr;
Content thy self with the small barren praise
Which neglected Verse does raise, &c.

However by the failing of the Forces which I had
expected, I did not quit the Design which I had
resolved on, I cast my self into it *A Corps Perdu*,
without making capitulations, or taking counsel of
Fortune. But God laughs at a Man, who sayes to his
Soul, *Take thy ease:* I met presently not onely with
many little encumbrances and impediments, but with
so much sickness (a new misfortune to me) as would
have spoiled the happiness of an Emperour as well as
Mine: Yet I do neither repent nor alter my course.
Non ego perfidum Dixi Sacramentum; Nothing shall
separate me from a Mistress, which I have loved so
long, and have now at last married; though she neither
has brought me a rich Portion, nor lived yet so quietly
with me as I hoped from Her.

——— *Nec vos, dulcissima mundi*
Nomina, vos Musæ, Libertas, Otia, Libri,
Hortique Sylvæq; anima remanente relinquam.

Nor by me ere shall you,
You of all Names the sweetest, and the best,
You Muses, Books, and Liberty and Rest;
You Gardens, Fields, and Woods forsaken be,
As long as Life it self forsakes not Me.

But this is a very petty Ejaculation; because I have
concluded all the other Chapters with a Copy of Verses,
I will maintain the Humour to the last.

Martial. L. 10. Ep. 47.

Vitam quæ faciunt beatiorem, &c.

SInce, dearest Friend, 'tis your desire to see
    A true Receipt of Happiness from Me;
These are the chief Ingredients, if not all;
Take an Estate neither too great nor small,
Which *Quantum Sufficit* the Doctors call.
Let this Estate from Parents care descend;
The getting it too much of Life does spend.
Take such a Ground, whose gratitude may be
A fair Encouragement for Industry.
Let constant Fires the Winters fury tame;
And let thy Kitchens be a Vestal Flame.
Thee to the Town let never Suit at Law;
And rarely, very rarely Business draw.
Thy active Mind in equal Temper keep,
In undisturbed Peace, yet not in sleep.
Let Exercise a vigorous Health maintain,
Without which all the Composition's vain.
In the same weight Prudence and Innocence take,
Ana of each does the just mixture make.
But a few Friendships wear, and let them be
By Nature and by Fortune fit for thee.
In stead of Art and Luxury in food,
Let Mirth and Freedome make thy Table good.
If any cares into thy Day-time creep,
At night; without Wines Opium, let them sleep.
Let rest, which Nature does to Darkness wed,
And not Lust, recommend to thee thy Bed,

T.C.E.   8

Be satisfi'd, and pleas'd with what thou art;
Act chearfully and well th' alotted part,
Enjoy the present Hour, be thankful for the Past,
And neither fear, nor wish th' approaches of the last.

Martial Book 10. *Epigram* 96.

ME who have liv'd so long among the great,
   You wonder to hear talk of a Retreat:
And a retreat so distant, as may show
No thoughts of a return when once I go.
Give me a Country, how remote so e're,
Where happiness a mod'rate rate does bear,
Where poverty it self in plenty flowes,
And all the solid use of Riches knowes.
The ground about the house maintains it there,
The House maintains the ground about it here.
Here even Hunger's dear, and a full board,
Devours the vital substance of the Lord.
The Land it self does there the feast bestow,
The Land it self must here to Market go.
Three or four suits one Winter here does wast,
One suit does there three or four winters last.
Here every frugal Man must oft be cold,
And little Luke-warm-fires are to you sold.
There Fire's an Element as cheap and free,
Almost as any of the other Three.
Stay you then here, and live among the Great, .
Attend their sports, and at their tables eat.
When all the bounties here of Men you score:
The Places bounty there, shall give me more.

Epitaphium Vivi Auctoris.

*H*Ic, *O Viator, sub Lare parvulo*
Couleius *Hic est Conditus, Hic Jacet;*
Defunctus humani Laboris
   Sorte, supervacuâque vitâ.
Non Indecorâ pauperie *Nitens,*
Et Non inerti *nobilis* otio,
   Vanóque dilectis popello
   Divitiis animosus hostis.
Possis ut illum dicere mortuum;
En Terra jam nunc Quantula *sufficit?*
   Exempta sit Curis, viator,
   Terra sit illa Levis, precare.
Hic sparge Flores, *sparge breves* Rosas,
Nam vita gaudet Mortua Floribus,
   Herbisque Odoratis Corona
   Vatis adhuc Cinerem Calentem.

Notes

PAGE **1**. A **Quit-Rent** is a rent, almost always of a very trifling amount, paid in respect of the tenure of an estate in fee-simple.

PAGE **2**. **Salust**. The quotation is from the speech of Lepidus against Sulla (ed. Teubner, p. 108). Cowley has substituted *vos* for *alios*.

Atalanta. She was the daughter of Iasus and Clymene. When her father wished her to marry, she made it a condition that she would accept the suitor who should conquer her in a footrace. Meilanion, who had obtained from Aphrodite three golden apples, dropped them on the course, and Atalanta, "fair as the snow and footed as the wind," stopped to pick them up and so was beaten.

Fertur &c. Virgil, *Georg.* I. 514, "The charioteer is borne on by his steeds, nor does the team heed the reins."

PAGE **3**. **nomenclator**, i.e. a person to announce the names of all whom the candidate met. Cowley in *The Mistress* says:

> Mean while I will not dare to *make* a *Name*
>> To represent thee by;
> *Adam* (*Gods nomenclator*) could not frame
>> One that enough should *signifie*.

The allusion is to *Romanos rerum dominos!* (*Aen.* I. 282).

the Beast with many heads, i.e. the populace.

Catiline. Lucius Sergius Catilina carried on a conspiracy against the Roman government for three years (B.C. 65–62), stirring up insurrections in Rome. Cicero attacked him in some of his finest speeches, and Sallust has left a history of his conspiracy.

Sylla's. Lucius Cornelius Sulla, who made himself dictator.

Machiavil. Niccolò Machiavelli (1469-1527) was a courageous and clear-sighted thinker, but in his *Prince* and other writings he upholds the pernicious doctrine that the State is not bound by the moral law.

this man &c. From Cicero, *pro Caelio*, V. 12–VI. 14.

PAGE **4**. **Above all things**. Note the length of this sentence.

laveer. This is a Dutch nautical word, and signifies "to sail in an oblique direction so as to catch the wind," and so fitly describes the action of a seeker after popular favour. It is used by Lovelace in a poem entitled Another (*Lucasta*, ed. Hazlitt, 1864, p. 209),

"Did on the shore himself *laveer.*"

And by Dryden, *Astræa Redux*, l. 65,

"But those that 'gainst stiff Gales *laveering* go
Must be at once resolv'd and skilful too."

PAGE 5. **immanity**, i.e. enormity.

an Anti-Paul. The very contrary of Paul. The Apostle "became all things to all men" that he might *save* some.

Salust. From *De Catilinae conjuratione*, chap. x.

Zopirus. The history of Zopirus is taken from Herodotus III. cc. 153–159.

PAGE 6. **Sufferance**, i.e. suffering, from French *souffrance.*

painful, i.e. painstaking. Cf. Fuller, *Holy State*, "The Learned, pious, and painfull Preacher" (William Perkins). Also Burton's *Anatomy*, "Let there be bountiful patrons, and there will be *painful* scholars in all sciences."

PAGE 7. **gotten.** This old form survives only in *ill-gotten*; it is used by Pope in his translation of the *Iliad.*

made free of a Royal Company. The metaphor of apprenticeship is carried on; "made a freeman of a chartered company." Later editions read *royal company*, omitting the *a*, which completely changes the meaning.

Seneca. From *De Consolatione, Ad Polybium*, VI. 26, "Magna servitus est magna fortuna."

to Atticus. From Cic. *Epist., Brutus*, I, 17. 4.

Groom. In the older sense of a man-servant.

PAGE 8. **Amatorem &c.** "Three hundred chains bind the lover Pirithous." From Horace, *Od.* III. 4. 79.

Aliena &c. From Horace, *Satires*, II. 6. 33 ff.

PAGE 9. **Dorres.** Cockchafers. Cf. Burton's *Anatomy*, "They shew their wit in censuring others, a company of foolish note-makers, humble-bees, *dors* or beetles."

Endeavourers. Used by Steele in the *Tatler.*

as the Scripture speakes. The allusion is to Ps. lxix. 23.

PAGE 10. **Pan huper sebastus**, i.e. πᾶν ὑπὲρ σεβαστός, "altogether superlatively august."

Hitherto &c. Job xxxviii. 11.

Perditur &c. From Horace, *Sat.* II. 6, 59.

impertinent. 'Aimless.'

Horace. The passage is a paraphrase of *Sat.* I. 6, 104–117.

cheapen, i.e. bargain for.

censure. The word has not always, as in modern English, the sense of 'blame,' 'rebuke.' Sometimes it means, as here, only 'opinion,' 'judgement.' Cf. Shakespeare, *Hamlet*, I. 3. 69,

"Take each man's *censure*, but reserve thy judgement."

PAGE **11. care of yours**, i.e. the care for those who are in your service.

Fasces, i.e. his rods, the instruments whereby he asserts his authority. The word used in Latin for the rods borne by a Roman lictor before a magistrate, indicating the power of summary punishment.

Epidemical, i.e. general.

a slave in Saturnalibus. The Roman Saturnalia, a feast in honour of Saturn, was held in December and lasted several days. During this time slaves were allowed full freedom of speech, and were treated as free men.

He heapeth &c. From Ps. xxxix. 6.

PAGE **12: Unciatim &c.** From Terence, *Phormio*, I. I. 43.

other. We should now say 'others.' But the form in the text as a plural was not uncommon.

κακὰ θηρία. The words are quoted from St Paul's Epistle to Titus, i. 12.

two directly opposite significations. ἀργός, derived from two distinct roots, has two meanings, (1) with πόδας = *swift-footed* (of dogs), (2) contracted from ἀεργός = *slow*.

Metrodorus. A Greek philosopher, disciple of Epicurus. The sentiment in the text is referred to more than once by Cicero; *De nat. deor.* I. 40; *Tusc. disput.* v. 9; *De fin.* II. 28[1].

PAGE **13. this World**. Note that *which* occurs three times in one short sentence.

Lepidus. M. Aemilius Lepidus, one of the second triumvirate with Antony and Octavius.

Quisnam &c. From Horace, *Sat.* II. 7. 83. "Who then is free? The wise man, and he who is able to control himself."

Oenomaus. King of Pisa, and father of Hippodameia. Not wishing his daughter to marry he compelled all her suitors to contend with him in a chariot-race. Having very swift horses he conquered many, but at last was overcome by the craft of Pelops.

PAGE **14. pour faire bonne bouche**, i.e. to serve as a tit-bit.

[1] Cowley has mistranslated the Greek, which means "truly to indulge the belly."

PAGE **16. Weathers**. The plural form is not very common. But cf. Shakespeare, *Winter's Tale*, v. 1. 195,

"Whose honesty endured all *weathers*."

the Persian king. The line in Martial says 'the Parthian king'; in his time Persia was under a Parthian dynasty.

the Freemans Hat. Among the Romans it was the custom to give a slave, on his enfranchisement, a cap, called *pileus*, to be worn as a sign of his liberty.

PAGE **17. Bridewell**. A house of correction for culprits. The name comes from St Bride's well in London, near which was a building used for this purpose.

PAGE **18. well-hung**, i.e. tapestried.

PAGE **19. Material**, i.e. embodied.

degenerous =degenerate. Cf. Fuller, *Holy State*, "The degenerous gentleman."

unbirdly. Formed after the analogy of *unmanly*.

Cornish Mount. St Michael's Mount.

PAGE **20. Rhodian Colossus**. This was a bronze statue of the Sun at Rhodes over 105 feet high and celebrated as one of the seven wonders of the world. It was the work of Chares, the favourite pupil of Lysippus, and was erected in B.C. 290. It was ruined by an earthquake 56 years later.

The Bondman of the Cloister, i.e. the monk.

hits the white. The white was the centre of the target.

PAGE **21. thorough**. For *through*. Cf. Shakespeare, *Pericles*, IV. 3. 35, "It pierced me *thorough*." Also 2 *Hen. IV*, I. 3. 59, "Who half *thorough* gives o'er."

a Compass take, i.e. go a roundabout road. 2 Sam. v. 23 (of an army); Acts xxviii. 13 (of sailing a vessel).

Nunquam &c., "One is never less alone than when alone." Quoted by Cicero, *De off.* III. 1 and *De republica*, I. 17.

vulgar, i.e. common.

PAGE **22. retired himself**. Shakespeare, *Winter's Tale*, IV. 4, "You must *retire yourself* into some covert."

Linternum. Generally called *Liternum*, a city of Campania. See Livy XXXVIII. 52 and 53.

Seneca. See Seneca, *Ep.* XIII. 1 (86).

colourably, i.e. plausibly.

Montagne. *Essais*, I. 38, "Respondons à l'ambition que c'est elle mesme qui donne goust de la solitude. Car que ne fuit-elle tant que la société?"

I, and Ushers too. I is the oldest form of *aye*. *Usher* is from *huissier* (Lat. *ostiarius*) = (1) a door-keeper (old), (2) one who walks before a person of rank, to announce him &c.

PAGE 23. Tecum &c. "With thee I should love to live. with thee I would gladly die," Horace, *Od.* III. 9. 24.

Sic ego &c. Tibullus IV. 13. 9.

conversation, i.e. communion with it.

Odi & Amo. From Catullus LXXXV.

to. A 17th century spelling of *too*.

Fop, i.e. fool, its original meaning.

PAGE 24. O vita. The sentence is from Publilius Syrus, *Sententiae*, 202. It should read "*O vita misero longa, felici brevis.*"

PAGE 25. divertisements, i.e. diversions.

PAGE 26. O quis me &c. Virgil, *Georg.* II. 489. "O that some one would set me down under the cool mountains of Haemus and shield me with a mighty shade of boughs." But Virgil wrote "O *qui* me gelidis *convallibus* Haemi."

PAGE 28. the, a 17th century spelling of *thee*.

thy Millions. The population of London at this time was less than half a million.

Nam neque &c. Horace, *Ep.* I. 17. 9.

PAGE 29. deceive. *Fallere* means not only "to deceive" but also "to escape notice" (as here), or (trans.) "to beguile." *Deceive* was sometimes used in the last sense.

Secretum &c. Horace, *Ep.* I. 18. 103.

Mr Broom. This was Alexander Broom (or Brome) born 1620, died 1666. His translation of Horace (with Ben Jonson, Cowley and others) was published in 1666.

same Authour. Horace, *Sat.* II. 7. 114.

Quintilian. *Declam.* XIII. *De Apibus Pauperis*.

amuse. In the older sense of occupy.

Bene qui &c. Ovid, *Trist.* III. 4. 25.

PAGE 30. A vail &c. The lines are translated from Virg. *Aen.* I. 412 f.

Fidus Achates has become proverbial.

Demosthenes's confession. The story is told by Cicero, *Tusc.* V. XXXVI. 103.

Tanker-woman, i.e. tankard-woman, a water-carrier.

sight-shot. A word modelled after the fashion of 'ear-shot.'

Democritus. The famous philosopher of Abdera, the originator of the atomic theory.

commodity. Advantage, profit. Cf. Shakespeare, *King John*, II. 1. 573,

> "That smooth-faced gentleman, tickling *Commodity*,
> *Commodity*, the bias of the world."

Metrodorus. See above p. 119.

one of his letters. The passage is a free rendering of Seneca, *Ep*. X. 3. 15.

commemoration, i.e. mention.

PAGE **31**. **Quotidian Ague**, i.e. a daily shivering fit.

St Peter. The reference is to Acts v. 15, "They brought forth the sick into the streets...that at least the shadow of Peter passing by might overshadow some of them."

Cato, i.e. Marcus Porcius Cato, known as Cato the Censor. He died B.C. 149.

Aristides. The famous Athenian statesman of the 5th cent. B.C. known as "The Just."

PAGE **32**. **commerce**, i.e. intercourse, as in French. Cf. Shakespeare, *Hamlet*, III. 1,

"Could. beauty, my lord, have better *commerce* than with honesty?"

askt with his last breath. Suet. *Aug*. 99, "Ecquid iis videretur mimum vitæ commode transegisse."

PAGE **33**. **O fortunatus &c.** O too fortunate man and one who knew his blessings. An adaptation of Virg. *Georg*. II. 458.

PAGE **34**. **Columella**. From *De re rustica*, I. 1. Columella lived in the 1st century A.D.

Varro. From *De re rustica*, I. 4. Varro (B.C. 116–28) was a man of great and various learning, but only his *De re rustica* survives in a complete form.

Cicero saies. *De Senectute*, XV. 51.

Ennius (B.C. 239–169) wrote an epic poem on Roman history; only fragments remain.

as they were in Rome. Alluding to the well-known stories of Cincinnatus and M'. Curius Dentatus. See Cicero, *De Senect*. XVI. 56.

PAGE **35**. **stock**, i.e. farm stock.

Tropes, i.e. metaphorical forms of expression. The word is from the Gk. τρόπος = *a turn*.

beholding. We now use 'beholden.' But the form in the text was common in the 17th century.

PAGE **37**. **instance in**. Cf. Sir W. Temple, *Letter to Lord Arlington*, July 1669:

"The Dutch desired the particular instances of what they had felt or thought they had occasion to fear: our merchants *instanced in* Cochin and Cananor."

Hinc atque hinc &c. Virg. *Aen*. I. 502.

NOTES

PAGE **38**. **Builder**. Cain, after Abel's murder, built the city of Enoch (Gen. iv. 17).

Ecclèsiasticus, vii. 15.

Fields d'Or, or d'Argent. The *field* is the ground of a shield. Its *tincture* may be a metal, a colour, or a fur. The metals are *or* =gold, and *argent* =silver.

Columella. See above.

PAGE **39**. **Principal**. The title of the head of a Hall at Oxford.

PAGE **40**. **Villaticas Pastiones**. Varro, *De re rustica*, 3. 2. 13.

Ostentation of Critical Literature, i.e. Parade of classical learning.

Mr Hartlib. Samuel Hartlib was a friend of Milton. He was of Polish extraction, but settled in England and wrote on education and agriculture. Milton dedicated to him his Tractate on Education.

T'has. A peculiar form for *'Thas*.

Nescio qua &c. Ovid, *Epist. ex Ponto*, 1. 3. 35.

PAGE **41**. **Pariter &c.** Ovid, *Fasti* I. 299 f., with *locis* for *jocis*.

Hesiod lived in the 8th century B.C.

He has contributed (sayes Columella). *De re rustica*, I. 1.

PAGE **42**. **Νήπιοι**. Hesiod, *Works and Days*, 40. "Childish ones who knew not how much more the half is than the whole, nor how great a profit there is in mallow and asphodel, for the gods keep life hidden from men."

his Father Laertes. See Hom. *Odyss.* XXIV. 226 ff.

PAGE **43**. **Eumæus**. *Ib.* XV. 301, and often.

Theocritus. *Idyll* XXV. 51 (spurious).

Civil, i.e. courteous.

describing Evander. See Virg. *Aen.* VIII.

Escurial. The great gloomy palace of the Escorial, about 25 miles from Madrid, was built by Philip II in fulfilment of a vow made at the battle of St Quentin (1557), when he implored the aid of St Laurence, on whose day it was fought. It was built in the form of a gridiron, in remembrance of the saint's martyrdom.

Whitehall. The palace of the Kings of England from Henry VIII to William III. Inigo Jones added to it the noble Banqueting House, which alone was preserved when the rest was destroyed by fire in January 1698. It was converted into a chapel in the reign of George I.

Alcides. Hercules, who was the grandson of Alceus. The lines are from *Aen.* VIII. 362 ff.

PAGE **44**. **ut nos &c.** Suetonius, *Vita Horati*, "that he may help us in writing letters."

Sabin, or Tiburtin Mannor. Horace was presented by Maecenas with a small Sabine farm situate at the village of Mandela (modern Bardella) on the river Digentia (modern Licenza), about 10 miles from Tibur. He afterwards bought or hired a villa at Tibur itself (the modern Tivoli).

Qui quid &c. "Who tells us more fully and better than Chrysippus and Crantor what is fair, what foul, what useful and what not so." From Horace, *Epist.* I. 2. 3. Chrysippus (b. 280 B.C.) was a Stoic philosopher, Crantor (*fl.* 300 B.C.) belonged to the Academy.

PAGE **45**. **Poyson of Assyrian pride**, i.e. Tyrian dyes. *Assyrian =Syrian.*

PAGE **46**. **Astræa**. The goddess of Justice (Virgil has *Justitia*), a fabled daughter of Jupiter and Themis.

PAGE **47**. **Tempe**. A valley of Thessaly, lying between Mt Ossa and Mt Olympus, watered by the river Peneus.

pop'ular fame. The apostrophe is used in the 1668 edition to mark the silence or slurring over of either the following or the preceding sound (Gough).

PAGE **48**. **Tyrian beds**. The luxury of Tyre was pro verbial.

drink in Gold, i.e. *out of* gold, from golden cups.

home, i.e. at home.

Wives =wife's.

Amidst his equal friends, i.e. friends of the same age. A common sense of the Latin *aequalis*.

PAGE **49**. **Let in the Sea &c.**, i.e. admitted the sea to share with earth the bringing about of their death. So Gough explains it, probably rightly, but the line is very obscure.

PAGE **50**. **Use**, i.e. profit. Cf. Selden, *Table Talk, usury*, "The Jews were forbidden to take *use* one of another."

PAGE **51**. **To pin** =to make fast.

against, i.e. until.

lustful, i.e. provocation of lust.

Ortalans nor Godwits. The ortolan, a native of most European countries, except the British isles, is a species of bunting, much resembling the yellow-hammer but less brightly coloured. The name is derived from *hortulanus*. The godwit is a marsh bird formerly abundant in Lincolnshire, Norfolk and the Isle of Ely, and highly prized as a delicacy. It is now only a visitor to this country (Newton, *A Dictionary of Birds*).

NOTES
125

Horace, *Sat.* II. VI. 79 ff. Cowley has much expanded his original. A third *locus classicus* on the pleasures of the country is the speech of Hippolytus in Seneca, *Phaedra*, 491 ff. Du Bartas (*La Semaine*, III. 897 ff.) was inspired by all three poets, his contemporary Desportes (*Œuvres*, p. 431) has written upon the same theme, and both were plagiarised by Racan in his poem, *Tircis, il faut penser à la Retraite.*

PAGE 52. **belighted**, a word formed on the analogy of *benighted.*

Fitches, i.e. vetches.

Peason, i.e. peas. A form of the old plural *pesen.*

The swerd of Bacon. 'Swerd' with the variants 'sword' and 'swarth' is applied to the outer skin of swine as well as to the grass-covered surface of the ground.

PAGE 53. **troth.** A variant of 'truth,' only found now in the phrases 'in troth,' and 'to plight one's troth.'

Mortclakes noble Loom. In the reign of King James I the manufacture of tapestry was set up at Mortlake in Surrey.

PAGE 54. **fraited**, i.e. freighted.

PAGE 55. 'The mad Celestial Dog' is Sirius the dog-star, which is in the ascendant when the hot weather called the dog-days prevails. 'The Lyon' is the sign of Leo. *Dogs* and *Lyons* are *gen. sing.*

PAGE 56. **right Gems**, i.e. genuine gems.

wan. An obsolete form for *won.*

PAGE 57. **Blest be the man &c.** These lines are a translation from Cowley's own Latin at the beginning of Bk. IV of his *Sex Libri Plantarum.*

whom e're. The apostrophe indicates the omission of *ve* (Gough).

PAGE 58. **The old Corycian Yeoman.** The allusion is to Virgil, *Georg.* IV. 127 ff.

Abdolonymus. A gardener of royal descent (Q. Curtius IV. 1). The 'great Emperour' was Alexander the Great, who made him king of Sidon.

Aglaüs, a poor man of Psophis in Arcadia. Gyges was king of Lydia. The story is told by Pliny, *H.N.* VII. 46, 151 and by Valerius Maximus VII. 1. 2.

PAGE 59. **Sopho's Town**, i.e. Psophis.

Earnest. A present pledge of something to happen in the future. Thus a quiet life here is to be the pledge of heavenly rest hereafter. Cf. Shakespeare, *Macbeth* I. 3,

> "And for an *earnest* of a greater honour
> He bade me call thee thane of Cawdor."

This essay is addressed to John Evelyn (1620–1706), the author of the famous *Diary*, first published in 1818–19, and of *Sylva* (1664). In 1664 he published his *Kalendarium Hortense* or *The Gardener's Almanac* and in 1666 he dedicated the second edition to his friend Cowley. This essay is Cowley's acknowledgement.

PAGE **60. Studiis &c.** "To flourish in the pursuits of inglorious leisure." From Virg. *Georg.* IV. 564.

Inn, a hired house, i.e. the Porch House, Chertsey.

O let me... Genesis xix. 20. Lot's prayer on his flight from Sodom.

Pindarical, i.e. highflown.

Chymist, i.e. alchemist, of which *chymist* or chemist is a shortened form.

affections = inclinations.

PAGE **61. to the main.** To have the chief part of the estate, i.e. to be specially distinguished above the rest of your literary progeny.

that Book, which you are pleased to Promise. Evelyn's *Compleat Gardener*, which he did not publish till 1693.

Expences, i.e. expenditure of time and trouble as well as money (Gough).

PAGE **62. Wife.** Evelyn married a daughter of Sir Richard Browne, the representative of Charles I and Charles II at the French Court.

PAGE **63. Escurial.** See above, p. 123.

the first City, i.e. Enoch. See above, p. 123.

PAGE **64. Base.** We now write *bass* from the French *basse*.

Arts Musick, i.e. musical instruments.

Theorbo. A double-necked lute with two sets of strings and tuning pegs; It. *tiorba*. See Evelyn's *Diary*, July 1, 1654, "At All Souls, where we had music, voices and theorbos, performed by some ingenious scholars." There is a portrait of a man with a theorbo by Vandyck in Lord Northbrook's collection.

See Virg. *Aen.* I. 691–694.

PAGE **65. Femal Men**, i.e. effeminate dandies.

Epicurus. See above, pp. 13 and 30. Cowley hints in the words which follow that Epicurus' meaning, when he called pleasure the chief good, ought to be interpreted by his definition of what pleasure is.

Vitellius, who succeeded as Otho as Roman Emperor in A.D. 69, was a notorious glutton. His table is called 'fiscal' because it taxed largely the resources of the whole empire for its supply.

listed, i.e. included in a list; it is recorded now as a modern Americanism.

the Third Story high. Because the dessert, consisting of fruits, formed the third course at dinner in Cowley's day.

PAGE 66. **the great Hebrew King**, i.e. Solomon. The allusions which follow are to his entertainment of the Queen of Sheba. See I Kings x.

Hiram's Princely Dy, i.e. Tyrian purple. Hiram was king of Tyre.

one that would not be so Rich. "Consider the lilies of the field...Even Solomon in all his glory was not arrayed like one of these" (Matt. vi. 29).

PAGE 67. The name *arbor vitae* has been given to trees of the genus *Thuja* or *Thuia*. *T. occidentalis*, the American *arbor vitae*, is frequently used for hedges.

PAGE 68. **intend**, i.e. strain. Cp. Lat. *oculum intendere*.

the Flowers of Heaven, i.e. the stars, just as the *Stars of Earth* are plants.

Grafs, graf or **graff** is the old form of *graft*. Evelyn uses this form of the verb and even Scott: "Why I scarce remember the pearmains which I graffed here with my own hands," says Abbot Boniface in the last chapter of *The Abbot*.

PAGE 69. **Galatea.** See Virg. *Ecl.* III. 64–72.

the savage Hawthorn. Savage (Fr. *sauvage*, Lat. *silvaticus*) = wild. The hawthorn was used as a stock for grafting pears and medlars and the wild plum for grafting peaches.

Daphne's coyness. The laurel (Gr. δαφνή) into which Daphne was changed to escape from Apollo (Ovid, *Met.* I. 452) was *Laurus nobilis*, our bay, upon which it would be impossible to graft a cherry. Cowley means *Prunus laurocerasus*, the common laurel.

Dioclesian. Emperor of Rome. He abdicated in A.D. 305, and lived in retirement at Salona in Dalmatia, near which place he had been born. Aurelius Victor (*Epit.* 54) relates the story of his being urged to resume the throne once more. To which he answered, "If you could see the vegetables planted by my hands at Salona, you would never think of urging such a petition." The remains of his magnificent palace are still to be seen at Spalato.

rod, i.e. rode.

PAGE 70. **Sieur de Montagn.** Montaigne begins *Essai* III. 7 (*De l'incommodité de la grandeur*) with "Puisque nous ne la pouvons atteindre, vengeons nous à en mesdire."

convinced, i.e. convicted. Cf. St John viii. 46, "Which of you *convinceth me of sin?*" (The R.V. reads *convicteth*.)

Dii bene fecerunt &c. Horace, *Sat.* I. 4. 17, "The gods have done well in making me of a poor and lowly mind."

PAGE **71**. **Bona Roba**. A term for a robust and handsome woman. Cf. Shakespeare, 2 *Hen. IV*, III. 2,

> "We knew where the *bona robas* were."

Parvula &c. Lucr. IV. 1158,

"A small, dwarfish woman is one of the Graces, all pure wit."

Seneca the Elder, father of the more famous Seneca, was famous as a rhetorician. The account of Senecio is in his *Suasoriarum Liber*, II. 17.

Horse-plums. The prefix 'horse' is added to various terms to indicate unusual size, as 'horse-radish,' 'horse-chestnut,' 'horse-laugh.'

Chiopins. From the Italian *cioppini*. A kind of high shoe worn by ladies. Spelt also 'chopine' and 'chippine.' Cf. Shakespeare, *Hamlet*, II. 2, "Your ladyship is nearer to heaven than when I saw you last, by the altitude of a *chopine*."

cognomentum. Using a longer word, instead of a short one, after the fashion of Senecio's mania.

the three hundred Lacedæmonians, at Thermopylae.

PAGE **72**. **burly** = blustering.

PAGE **73**. **little singing Birds**. The allusion is to Louis XIII of France.

gods too. Because after death they were styled *divus*.

in catching of Flies. This is said by Suetonius to have been the frequent occupation of the Emperor Domitian.

bodkin, i.e. a *stilus*, a pointed iron instrument for writing on waxed tablets.

Beelzebub. The name signifies 'lord of flies.'

Alas &c. Qualis artifex pereo! (Suet. *Nero*, 49).

PAGE **74**. **Bounding-stones**, translation of *ocellata*, small stones marked like dice (Suet. *Aug.* 83).

Cates, i.e. dainties.

PAGE **75**. **Forest-work hangings**, i.e. tapestry.

Sed quantum &c. Virg. *Georg.* II. 291.

PAGE **76**. **Cousinage**. We write now *cozenage* = cheating.

Mancipiis &c. Horace, *Epist.* I. 6. 39, "The king of the Cappadocians, rich in slaves, lacks coin."

says Solomon. Eccl. V. 11, "When goods increase, they are increased that eat them."

like Ocnus in the Fable. The reference is to a picture by Polygnotus, mentioned by Pausanias X. 29. 2, and by Pliny, *Hist. Nat.* XXXV. 11, 137.

PAGE **77**. **Pic of Tenarif**. The French form of the word, *Pic*, had not in Cowley's time given place to the English *Peak*.

the late Gyant of our Nation, i.e. Oliver Cromwell.

PAGE **78**. **an Idol is nothing in the World**. 1 Cor. viii. 4.

like Cæsar. The saying is recorded by Plutarch, *Caesar*, XI, but it was probably suggested to Cowley by Montaigne, who in the Essay quoted from above says, "Tout à l'opposite de l'autre m'aymerois à l'avanture mieux, deuxiesme ou troisiesme à Paris."

this whole Globe &c. Hurd compares Addison in the *Spectator*, nos. 420 and 565, and Pascal, *Pensées*, "Que l'homme contemple donc la nature entière dans sa haute et pleine majesté;...qu'il regarde cette éclatante lumière mise comme une lampe éternelle pour éclairer l'univers; que la terre lui paraisse comme un point, au prix du vaste tour que cet astre décrit, et qu'il s'étonne de ce que ce vaste tour lui-même, n'est qu'un point très délicat à l'égard de celui que les astres qui roulent dans le firmament embrassent." Pascal has evidently been inspired here by Montaigne I. 25, who uses the very words, "pointe très délicate," and it is a fairly safe conjecture that Cowley is indebted to the same source.

PAGE **79**. **Damocles**. The 'sword of Damocles' is proverbial. For the story see Cicero, *Tusc*. V. 21.

PAGE **80**. **two Comets**. Cowley is perhaps referring to the comets of December 1664 and April 1665 (Gough).

Let Mars and Saturn...conjoyn. An allusion to the supposed influence of the stars on the fortunes of mankind. The conjunction of Mars and Saturn might portend war and other calamities, but the beneficent influence of Jove within a man's heart makes him superior to all external powers.

PAGE **81**. **refunding**. In the literal sense of the Lat. *refundere*, 'to pour back again.'

excern. To excrete.

Chough. The word was used in Cowley's time of any of the smaller crow tribe, especially of a jackdaw. The true Cornish chough has red legs.

PAGE **82**. **Desunt &c.** Cowley is mistaken in assigning these words to Ovid. They are found in the *Controversiae* of the elder Seneca, VII. 3.

Some body sayes. Sir Henry Wotton in his *Character of a Happy Life*.

Antipode. The use of this word in the singular was formerly common.

Audivi eos &c. Terence, *Eunuchus* IV. iii. 23.

T.C.E.   9

PAGE **83**. **Horace's first Satyre**, I. i. 1–79.

PAGE **84**. **Pismire**, i.e. an ant.

strait, i.e. straightway.

PAGE **86**. **At unawares**. *Unawares* is an old adverbial genitive: *at* is redundant.

as if thou &c., i.e. As if thou wert merely a collector of coins.

PAGE **87**. **Elixar**. An obsolete form of *elixir*.

The prudent Macedonian King. Philip of Macedon, father of Alexander the Great, boasted that no town was impregnable into which an ass laden with gold could be introduced (Cicero, *ad Atticum* I. 16. 12).

Petar. We now write 'petard.' Cf. Shakespeare, *Hamlet*, III. 4,

"To have the engineer hoist with his own *petar*."

PAGE **88**. **The vast Xerxean Army**. Cowley compares towns and courts, with their crowds, to the army which Xerxes led to Thermopylae, and which is said by Herodotus to have numbered 5,283,220—evidently an enormous exaggeration. These were resisted in the pass of Thermopylae by Leonidas, king of Sparta, with a small army, numbering 5200, of whom 300 were Spartans. These the poet compares to the poor who "hold the straights (i.e. straits) of poverty."

Sellars, i.e. cellars.

PAGE **89**. **Cap a pe**, now written cap-à-pie, from Old Fr. *cap a pie*, 'head to foot.' The modern Fr. form is *de pied en cap*.

Campagn. The level plain country. It. *campagna*; Fr. *campagne*.

PAGE **90**. **Toupinambaltians**. The habits and customs of this tribe, which dwelt in northern Brazil, and especially their barbarous treatment of their prisoners, are recorded by Jean de Lévy, a Protestant minister who joined Villegagnon's ill-fated colony in Brazil and published an account of his experiences in 1578. See c. XV of the Latin translation, *Historia Navigationis in Brasiliam*, 1586, which is no doubt Cowley's ultimate source, for Lévy contends that the Brazilian savages are less cruel than either the usurers of his own country or those who took part in the massacres of St Bartholomew. The same thought is repeated by Montaigne in his essay *On Cannibals*, I. 30. *Topinambous* is used by Boileau for (1) a savage tribe generally ("Est-ce chez les Herons, chez les Topinambous"), (2) a person of no taste ("L'Académie...me semble une peu topinamboue"). From the Topinambous comes also the French name for the Jerusalem artichoke—*topinambour*.

PAGE **91**. **Topick**. A general idea. The word comes from the Gk. τόποι, which Cicero (*Top.* II. 8) translates by *loci*.

Go to &c. Gen. xi. 4.

a concourse of Theives. Romulus offered an asylum to all those who from other places chose to take refuge with him. The other allusions in the sentence are to the birds seen by Romulus and Remus when they were looking for omens at the foundation of the city, and to the slaying of Remus by his brother. See Livy I. cc. VII and VIII.

first Town. See above, p. 123.

PAGE **92**. **at all pieces**. We now say 'at all points.'

Quid Romæ &c. "What can I do at Rome? I know not how to lie." From Juv. *Sat.* III. 41.

PAGE **93**. **Honest and Poor &c.** Martial, *Ep.* IV. 5.

Beldams, i.e. aged women. *Beldam* (from *bel*, a prefix used to express relationship and *dam* = mother) meant originally 'a grandmother' or 'a great-grandmother.'

Lucretius. The reference is to Lucr. II. 1,

"Suave mari magno turbantibus aequora ventis
E terra magnum alterius spectare laborem."

Democritus. The philosopher of Abdera who flourished about 430 B.C. He was famed among other things for looking at the cheerful side of life, and so was known as "the laughing philosopher." Hence the wrong idea of later writers that "he laughed at all the world."

Bedlam, i.e. the hospital of St Mary of Bethlehem, which became a madhouse in 1402.

PAGE **94**. **Ut nec facta &c.** A favourite quotation of Cicero's, said by some to be from the *Pelops* of Accius.

qua terra patet &c. "Far as the land extends the fierce Fury reigns. You would suppose they had sworn allegiance to crime." Ovid, *Met.* I. 241.

as the Scripture speaks. 2 Kings xvii. 17.

PAGE **95**. **Sir Phil. Sydney**. His pastoral romance, *The Countess of Pembroke's Arcadia*, was published posthumously in 1590 and had an enormous popularity.

Monsieur d'Urfe. Honoré d'Urfé (1567–1625) wrote a pastoral romance called *L'Astrée* (1607–1619) which was no less popular than the *Arcadia*. The scene is laid on the river Lignon, a tributary of the Loire in La Forest, where the author lived.

Chertsea. *Chertsey* is a small town in Surrey, on the Thames, where Cowley retired in 1665.

132 NOTES

St Pauls advice. 1 Cor. vii. 29.

Mundum ducere. In Latin, when a man marries he s said uxorem *ducere*, i.e. to lead a wife; whereas the woman was said marito *nubere*, to veil for her husband, and thus to admit his superiority.

PAGE 96. The passage is from Claudian, *Epigrammata* II. He flourished *c*. A.D. 400.

propension, i.e. stooping.

Benacus. The modern Lago di Garda.

a third age. That is, he lives to see his grandchildren.

PAGE 97. **Pas de Vie.** The Straits of life, as the Straits of Dover are called the *Pas de Calais*.

Pindar. *Pythian* VIII. 135.

our Saviour bounds our desires. By teaching us to pray only for *daily* bread. Also (Matth. vi. 34) "Take no thought for the morrow."

Tam brevi &c. Adapted from Horace, *Odes* II. 16. 17.

Millenaries. The Millenarians, or Chiliasts, believed that Christ would come to reign with His saints a thousand years upon earth. Their notion was founded upon Rev. xx. 4–6.

PAGE 98. **as we are taught.** Psalm xc. 12.

spatio brevi &c. The passage, which is translated in the next line, is from *Odes* I. 11. 6.

Vitæ summa &c. From *Odes* I. 4. 15, "The short sum of life forbids us to form a long hope."

Oh quanta &c. "Oh, how great is the madness of those who form long hopes." From Seneca, *Ep.* XVII. i. 4.

Senecio. A different man to the Senecio referred to on p. 71.

PAGE 99. **Insere &c.** Virg. *Ecl.* I. 73.

graff. See above, p. 127.

St Luke, xii. 16–20.

PAGE 101. **Husband.** In the old sense of a thrifty person. Cf. Shakespeare, *Taming of the Shrew* v. 1, "While I play the good *husband* at home, my son and my servant spend all."

travail, i.e. travel.

PAGE 102. **Nature had so Motherly inclined me.** Cf. Montaigne III. 13, "Nature a maternellement observé cela."

PAGE 103. **Ærugo mera**, i.e. pure rust. Cp. Scott, *The Antiquary*, c. XI: "But me no buts."

Idomeneus. A native of Lampsacus, and a disciple and friend of Epicurus. The passage translated is from Seneca, *Ep.* II. 9.

PAGE 104. **Utere velis.** Juvenal I. 149, Use the sails, spread all the canvas."

beaten up, i e. attacked.

Band, i.e. collar.

Festina lente, "Hasten slowly."

Sapere Aude. Horace, *Epist.* I. 2. 40. Cowley has substituted *labitur* for *defluat*, but gives the sense of *defluat* in his translation.

Portam &c. From Varro, *De re rustica*, I. 2. 2.

PAGE **105. Jam Cras &c.** Persius, *Sat.* V. 68. Persius was a Roman satirist of the time of Nero.

PAGE **106. Triary.** *Triarii*, i.e. the soldiers in a Roman army who formed the third rank and so acted as reserves.

you who instruct the Town. The epigram is addressed to Quintilian, the famous teacher of rhetoric.

preposterous. In the literal sense of the Lat. *praeposterus*: reversing the order of things, putting the last first.

PAGE **107. nice**, i.e. delicate.

grates, i.e. grates upon.

affections, i.e. disposition.

PAGE **108. dispensed with me**, i.e. granted me a dispensation.

an Ode. The verses quoted are from *A Vote*, i.e. a Prayer, a poem included in Cowley's *Sylva* published in 1636. Cowley has made a few changes, but *unknown* for *ignote* (l. 5) and *have* for *hug* are the only ones of any importance.

PAGE **109. Sabine.** See above, p. 124.

out of Horace. *Od.* III. 29. 41–45.

PAGE **110. violent Publick storm.** Cowley left Cambridge in 1643.

one of the best Persons. Lord Jermyn, afterwards Earl of St Albans. (See Introduction.)

one of the best Princesses. Queen Henrietta Maria.

PAGE **111. rid**, i.e. rode. Cowley also uses *rod* (see above, p. 127).

Well then. This poem is from Cowley's *Mistress*, and is entitled *The Wish*.

PAGE **112. Thou, neither great.** The extract is from *Destinie*, one of Cowley's *Pindarick Odes*.

quit. Later editions read *acquit*, which gives the exactly opposite sense to that intended by Cowley.

A Corps Perdu, i.e. headlong.

Take thy ease. St Luke xii. 16–21.

Non ego &c. Hor. *Od.* II. 17. 9, "I have not sworn a faithless oath."

Nec vos &c. The lines are probably Cowley's own. For *hortique* read, to make the line scan, *Vos, horti*.

PAGE **113**. **Quantum Sufficit**, i.e. just sufficient. Abbreviated in medical prescriptions to *quant. suff.*

a Vestal Flame. A repetition of the idea 'Let constant fires' in the previous line. The fire on the altar of Vesta was kept always burning.

Ana. A term in use in medical prescriptions to signify equal quantities of any ingredients. From Greek ἀνά = throughout.

PAGE **114**. **score**, i.e. count up.

PAGE **115**. **Hic, O Viator &c.** "Here wayfarer, beneath a little roof, here Cowley lies buried, discharged from the lot of human labour and from a useless life. He throve in honourable poverty, he was ennobled by active leisure, and was a bold foe to wealth beloved of the idle populace. That you may know him to be dead, see how small a plot of earth now suffices him! Pray, wayfarer, that this earth may be free from cares and lie lightly on him. Here strew flowers, strew short-lived roses, for a life that is dead delights in flowers, and crown with fragrant herbs the still warm ashes of the bard."

Index to the Notes

For EU product safety concerns, contact us at Calle de José Abascal, 56–1°, 28003 Madrid, Spain or eugpsr@cambridge.org.

www.ingramcontent.com/pod-product-compliance
Ingram Content Group UK Ltd.
Pitfield, Milton Keynes, MK11 3LW, UK
UKHW012332130625
459647UK00009B/230